THE GREAT EVANGELICAL DISASTER

By *Francis A. Schaeffer*

The God Who Is There
Escape from Reason
He Is There and He Is Not Silent
Death in the City
Pollution and the Death of Man
The Church at the End of the 20th Century
The Mark of the Christian
The Church Before the Watching World
True Spirituality
Basic Bible Studies
Genesis in Space and Time
The New Super-Spirituality
Back to Freedom and Dignity
Art and the Bible
No Little People
Two Contents, Two Realities
Joshua and the Flow of Biblical History
No Final Conflict
How Should We Then Live?
Whatever Happened to the Human Race?
    (with *C. Everett Koop*)
A Christian Manifesto
The Complete Works of Francis Schaeffer
    (including all the above titles in five volumes)
Everybody Can Know (with *Edith Schaeffer*)
The Great Evangelical Disaster

THE GREAT EVANGELICAL DISASTER

by

Francis A. Schaeffer

CROSSWAY BOOKS • WESTCHESTER, ILLINOIS
A Division of Good News Publishers

PERMISSIONS AND APPRECIATION

The publisher would like to express special appreciation to those who assisted in doing research for this volume, especially to Melinda Delahoyde, Director of Education for the Americans United for Life, and to Jonathan D. Lauer, Head of Public Services for the Wheaton College Library.

The publisher also would express special thanks to Denise Gill for her excellent work in typing the manuscript for the book—sometimes on a few minutes notice, often late at night, but always with a very professional and willing spirit.

Finally, the publisher would like to express appreciation for permission to quote from the following:

The Mark of the Christian, by Francis A. Schaeffer, copyright © 1970 by Francis A. Schaeffer, used by permission of InterVarsity Press, Downers Grove, Illinois 60515. *The Mark of the Christian* is available from InterVarsity Press as a separate booklet.

The *Holy Bible: New International Version*, copyright © 1978 by the New York International Bible Society. Used by permission of Zondervan Bible Publishers. All Scripture quotations are taken from this translation of the Bible.

Who Is for Peace? by Francis A. Schaeffer, copyright © 1983 by Francis A. Schaeffer, used by permission of Thomas Nelson Publishers, Nashville, Tennessee.

Some of the material in Chapter Two previously appeared in print in a different form in *Action* magazine, Fall 1976, a publication of the National Association of Evangelicals.

The Great Evangelical Disaster. Copyright © 1984
by Francis A. Schaeffer. Published by Crossway Books,
a division of Good News Publishers, Westchester, Illinois 60153.

Cover design: The Cioni Artworks/Ray Cioni

First printing, 1984

Printed in the United States of America

Library of Congress Catalog Card Number 83-73125

ISBN 0-89107-309-4 (cloth edition)
ISBN 0-89107-308-6 (paperback edition)

To a new, young generation—
and to those in the older generation—
who will stand and be counted
as radicals for truth and for Christ.

Contents

Acknowledgment 9
Preface 11
The Relationship of the Film and Book 15

Part I: Introduction

1   What Really Matters? 19

Part II: The Watershed of the Evangelical World

2   Marking the Watershed 43
3   The Practice of Truth 67

Part III: Names and Issues

4   Connotations and Compromise 95
5   Forms of the World Spirit 111
6   The Great Evangelical Disaster 141

Part IV: Conclusion

7   Radicals for Truth 149

Part V: Appendix

8   The Mark of the Christian 155
Notes 183

Acknowledgment

As some of you will know, for seven weeks following Thanksgiving Day, 1983, I was critically ill. I was taken first to the hospital in Aigle, Switzerland, and then, after a literally life and death dash across the Atlantic as a stretcher case, I spent the major part of the next six weeks in St. Mary's Hospital, connected with Mayo Clinic. While in St. Mary's, Edith and our children were told three times that I was expected to die. Happily that time has passed. And as I write this now I am convalescing in one of the houses of the Rochester, Minnesota branch of L'Abri.

Thus, that seven weeks was totally snatched from my life along with most of the work I had hoped to do. In that situation this book never would have made the deadline for the seminars bearing the same name, if it had not been for the long hours and devotion of Lane Dennis, vice-president and general manager of Crossway Books.

Lane is a friend, and one who knows my work "forward

and backwards.'' He is the publisher of my *Complete Works* and *A Christian Manifesto*. He brought his whole family to spend three months at L'Abri in the summer of 1978. He has listened to many hours of my tapes, and he wrote his Ph.D. dissertation as a sociological study of L'Abri.

When I got out of the hospital I found that the seven weeks when I was in the hospital had not been lost. During this time Lane had been working long hours doing research and preparing my materials for the final manuscript. Thus, when a little time had passed and I felt a bit better, the manuscript was in a form ready for me to work. As I write this, we are still spending long hours on the phone and exchanging the last phases of the manuscript by Federal Express. There is every reason to believe now that the book will soon be on the Crossway presses and ready for the seminars as they begin early in March.

But the point is, if it had not been for Lane Dennis none of this would have been possible.

Nothing like this has ever occurred with my previous books and I, and everyone helped by the book, owe a debt of gratitude to Lane Dennis.

FRANCIS A. SCHAEFFER
February 7, 1984

Preface

As you begin reading this book, I would like to mention that I have something of a dilemma, and I have had this now for a number of years. Let me try to explain what this is: During the last two decades I have written twenty-three books. My early books dealt especially with the intellectual questions of philosophy and matters in the area of culture. Then there were the books dealing with the Christian life and the church. More recently my books have dealt especially with the area of civil needs and the needs of law and government.

Throughout all of my work there is a common unifying theme, which I would define as "the Lordship of Christ in the totality of life." If Christ is indeed Lord, he must be Lord of all of life—in spiritual matters, of course, but just as much across the whole spectrum of life, including intellectual matters and the areas of culture, law, and government. I would want to emphasize from beginning to end throughout my work the importance of evangelism (helping men and women come to know Christ as Savior), the need to walk daily with the Lord, to study God's Word, to live a life of prayer, and to show forth the love, compassion, and holiness of our Lord. But we must emphasize equally and at the same time the need to live this out in every area of culture and society.

This book which you are reading now needs to be seen, then, within the context of my work as a whole. My dilemma is that many will not have had the opportunity to be familiar with the full range of my work, and it would be impossible to review or cover all of this within the pages of this book.

At the same time, however, this book stands on its own, in speaking to the critical issues of the day. Thus, for the person reading my work for the first time this book really does provide a good place to begin. On the other hand, those who are already familiar with my work should see that this new book grows out of the critical situation in which we live today, but also that it is a direct extension and application of what I have written over the years.

And if you find what I say in these pages interesting and helpful, I would encourage you to go back and study through my earlier work. This is now available in a five-volume set of my *Complete Works,* published by Crossway Books. The set is arranged so as to best follow the flow of my thought, and it includes twenty-one of my books, revised throughout for this new edition, with a comprehensive index.

One of the purposes of this present book was to reaffirm and restate some of the ideas and themes from my earlier work, as well as to make extensions and application of these to the situation in which we live today. The notes at the end of the book should be consulted to see where in my other works many of these themes and ideas are developed in greater detail. I would also mention that my booklet *The Mark of the Christian* has been included as an appendix to this volume. I would ask you to read the rest of this book first, but also read *The Mark of the Christian*, since the principles expressed in this booklet will be needed especially in the difficult days that lie ahead. I am grateful to InterVarsity Press for granting permission to include this here, and would mention that this is also available from InterVarsity as a separate publication.

Finally I would say that the statement which I am making in the pages of this book is perhaps the most important statement I have ever written. It concerns what I call "The Great Evangelical Disaster" and the greatest problem we who are Christians face in our generation.

FRANCIS A. SCHAEFFER
February 1984

The Relationship of the
Film and the Book

An animated film entitled *The Great Evangelical Disaster* has been
made by my son Franky Schaeffer to accompany this book. The
film is a satire which speaks to those who are "outside" the
evangelical world, in the hope they will awaken to where modern Man has come. The film also speaks to Christians, to help
them realize how destructive the world spirit about us really is.
(The film is produced by Franky Schaeffer V Productions, and
distributed by Word, Inc., Waco, Texas. For more information,
see the back cover of this book.)

My book hopes to help evangelical Christians see how
much of evangelicalism has been accommodating to the destructive and ugly world spirit of our day; and to help young Christian radicals, and others, to stand courageously against this
accommodation.

I would also mention Franky Schaeffer's new book *Bad*

News For Modern Man (Crossway Books, Westchester, Illinois, 1984). This book is directly related to the film and the three projects constitute a unit.

The following page is a color reproduction of one of the scenes in the film. This will help you see something of the technique used in the film.

FRANCIS A. SCHAEFFER

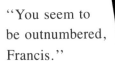

"You seem to
be outnumbered,
Francis."

PART I:

INTRODUCTION

CHAPTER 1

What Really Matters?

Time magazine recently published a special sixtieth anniversary edition with the title "The Most Amazing 60 Years." In recalling the world into which *Time* was born, this special issue began with the words: "The atom was unsplit. So were most marriages."[1] Here two things occurring in our era are properly brought together — one, the scientific technological explosion; and two, a moral breakdown. It is not just by accident that these two things have happened simultaneously. There is something which lies behind both phenomena, and in recognizing this *Time* really has shown amazing comprehension.

The Quest for Autonomy
Something happened during the last sixty years—something which cut the moral foundation out from under our culture. Devastating things have come in every area of culture, whether it be law or

government, whether it is in the schools, our local communities or in the family. And these have happened within the lifetime of many who are reading this book. Our culture has been squandered and lost, and largely thrown away. Indeed, to call it a moral breakdown puts it mildly. Morality itself has been turned on its head with every form of moral perversion being praised and glorified in the media and the world of entertainment.

How can we make sense of what has happened? In the main essay of this special edition *Time* offers an explanation. The essay, entitled "What really mattered?" suggests: "To determine what really mattered in this jumble [of events] seems to require a sense of something beyond the particulars." We will need, *Time* says, to discover the "idea characterizing [our] age."[2]

Time is quite right in this. In order to make sense of these last sixty years, and equally in order to understand the present and how we as Christians are to live today, we will need to understand the idea of our age—or what we might call the spirit of the times which has transformed our culture so radically since the 1920s. This idea, this spirit, *Time* says, has been the idea of "freedom"—not just freedom as an abstract ideal, or in the sense of being free from injustice, but *freedom in an absolute sense:*

> The fundamental idea that America represented corresponded to the values of the times. America was not merely free; it was freed, unshackled. The image was of something previously held in check, an explosive force of a country that moved about in random particles of energy yet at the same time gained power and prospered. To be free was to be modern; to be modern was to take chances. The American century was to be the century of unleashing, of breaking away, at first from the 19th century (as Freud, Proust, Einstein and

others had done), *and eventually from any constraints at all.*[3]

Further along in the same essay *Time* comments: "Behind most of these events lay the assumption, almost a moral *imperative, that what was not free ought to be free, that limits were intrinsically evil,*" and that science should go wherever it pleases in a spirit of "self-confident autonomy."[4] But, as *Time* concludes, "when people or ideas are unfettered, they are freed but not yet free."[5]

Form and Freedom

Here the problem of the 1920s to the 1980s is properly spelled out. It is the attempt to have absolute freedom—to be totally autonomous from any intrinsic limits. It is the attempt to throw off anything that would restrain one's own personal autonomy. But it is especially a direct and deliberate rebellion against God and his law.

In this essay *Time* has given that which indeed is central, namely the problem of form and freedom. It is a problem which every culture from the beginning of history has had to confront. The problem is this: If there is not a proper balance between form and freedom, then the society will move into either of two extremes. Freedom, without a proper balance of form, will lead to chaos and to the total breakdown of society. Form, without a proper balance of freedom, will lead to authoritarianism, and to the destruction of individual and social freedom. But note further: no society can exist in a state of chaos. And whenever chaos has reigned for even a short time, it has given birth to the imposition of arbitrary control.

In our own country we have enjoyed enormous human freedom. But at the same time this freedom has been founded upon forms of government, law, culture, and social morality which have given stability to individual and social life, and have kept our freedoms from leading to chaos. There is a balance here between form and freedom which we have come to take as natural in the world. But it is not natural. And we are utterly foolish if we do not recognize that this unique balance which we have inherited from the Reformation thought-forms is not automatic in a fallen world. This is clear when we look at the long span of history. But it is equally clear when we read the daily newspaper and see half the world locked in totalitarian oppression.

The Reformation not only brought forth a clear preaching of the gospel, it also gave shape to society as a whole—including government, how people viewed the world, and the full spectrum of culture. In Northern Europe, and in the countries such as the United States that are extensions of Northern Europe, the Reformation brought with it an enormous increase in knowledge of the Bible which spread through every level of society. This is not to say that the Reformation was ever a "golden age" or that everyone in the Reformation countries were true Christians. But it is clear that through the Reformation many were brought to Christ and that the absolutes of the Bible became widely disseminated in the culture as a whole. The freedoms which grew out of this were tremendous; and yet, with the forms grounded in a biblical consensus or ethos,[6] the freedoms did not lead to chaos.

But something has happened in the last sixty years. The freedom that once was founded on a biblical consensus and a Christian ethos has now become autonomous freedom, cut loose from all constraints. Here we have the world spirit of our age—autonomous Man setting himself up as God, in defiance of the knowledge and the moral and spiritual truth which God has given. Here is the reason why we have a moral breakdown in every area of life. The titanic freedoms which we once enjoyed have been cut loose from their Christian restraints and are becoming a force of destruction leading to chaos. And when this happens, there really are very few alternatives. All morality becomes relative, law becomes arbitrary, and society moves toward disintegration. In personal and social life, compassion is swallowed up by self-interest. As I have pointed out in my earlier books, when the memory of the Christian consensus which gave us freedom within the biblical form is increasingly forgotten, a manipulating authoritarianism will tend to fill the vacuum. At this point the words "right" and "left" will make little difference. They are only two roads to the same end; the results are the same. An elite, an authoritarianism as such, will gradually force form on society so that it will not go into chaos—and most people would accept it.[7]

The Battle We Are In

As evangelical, Bible-believing Christians we have not done well in understanding this. The world spirit of our age rolls on and on claiming to be autonomous and crushing all that we cherish in its path. Sixty years ago could we have imagined that unborn children would be killed by the millions here in our own country? Or that we would have *no freedom of speech* when it comes to speaking of God and biblical truth in our public schools? Or that every form of sexual perversion would be promoted by the entertainment media? Or that marriage, raising children, and family life would be objects of attack? Sadly we must say that very few Christians have understood the battle that we are in. Very few have taken a strong and courageous stand against the world spirit of this age as it destroys our culture and the Christian ethos that once shaped our country.

But the Scriptures make clear that we as Bible-believing Christians are locked in a battle of cosmic proportions. It is a life and death struggle over the minds and souls of men for all eternity, but it is equally a life and death struggle over life on this earth. On one level this is a spiritual battle which is being fought in the heavenlies. Paul's letter to the Ephesians presents the classic expression:

> For our struggle is not against flesh and blood, but against the rulers, against the authorities, against the powers of this dark world and against the spiritual forces of evil in the heavenly realms. (Ephesians 6:12)

Do we really believe that we are engaged in this cosmic battle? Do we really believe that there are "powers of this dark world" which rule our age? Or as the Apostle John says, do we really believe that "the whole world is under the control of the evil one" (1 John 5:19)? If we do not believe these things (and we must say that much of the evangelical world acts as if it does not believe these things), we certainly cannot expect to have much success in fighting the battle. Why has the Christian ethos in our culture been squandered? Why do we have so little impact upon the world today? Is it not because we have failed to take the primary battle seriously?

And if we have failed to take the battle seriously, we have certainly failed to use the weapons our Lord has provided. As the Apostle Paul writes:

> Finally, be strong in the Lord and in his mighty power. Put on the full armor of God so that you can take your stand against the devil's schemes . . . Therefore put on the full armor of God, so that when the day of evil comes, you may be able to stand your ground, and after you have done everything, to stand. Stand firm then, with the belt of truth buckled around your waist, with the breastplate of righteousness in place, and with your feet fitted with the readiness that comes from the gospel of peace. In addition to all this, take up the shield of faith, with which you can extinguish all the flaming

arrows of the evil one. Take the helmet of salvation and the sword of the Spirit, which is the word of God. And pray in the Spirit on all occasions with all kinds of prayers and requests. With this in mind, be alert and always keep on praying for all the saints. (Ephesians 6:10, 11, 13-18)

Note that there is nothing in this list that the world accepts as a way of working, but there is no other way to fight the spiritual battle in the heavenlies. And if we do not use these weapons we have no hope of winning.

The primary battle is a spiritual battle in the heavenlies. But this does not mean, therefore, that the battle we are in is otherworldly or outside of human history. It is a real spiritual battle, but it is equally a battle here on earth in our own country, our own communities, our places of work and our schools, and even our own homes. The spiritual battle has its counterpart in the visible world, in the minds of men and women, and in every area of human culture. In the realm of space and time the heavenly battle is fought on the stage of human history.

But if we are to win the battle on the stage of human history, it will take a prior commitment to fighting the spiritual battle with the only weapons that will be effective. It will take a life committed to Christ, founded on truth, lived in righteousness and grounded in the gospel. It is interesting to note that all of the weapons which Paul lists up to this point are defensive. The only offensive weapon mentioned is "the sword of the Spirit, which is the word of God." While the others help to defend us against the attacks of Satan, the Bible is the weapon which enables us to join with our Lord on the offensive in defeating the spiritual hosts of wickedness. But it must be the Bible as the Word of God in *everything it teaches*—in matters of salvation, but just as much where it speaks of history and science and morality. If it is compromised in any of these areas, as is unhappily happening today among many who call themselves evangelicals, we destroy the power of the Word and put ourselves in the hands of the enemy. Finally, it will take a life of prayer: "pray in the spirit on all occasions."

On the level of human history, however, the battle is equally important. Here too there is a fundamental conflict going on which is the earthly counterpart to the heavenly battle. This conflict takes two forms. The first of these has to do with the way we think — the ideas we have and the way we view the world. The second has to do with the way we live and act. Both of these conflicts— in the area of ideas and in the area of actions — are important; and in both areas Bible-believing Christians find themselves locked in battle with the surrounding culture of our day.

The Wisdom of the World
The battle in the area of ideas is pointed out most clearly in the letters of the Apostle Paul.[8] Here we see that there is a fundamental conflict between "the wisdom of this world" and "the wisdom of God." Thus Paul writes:

> Where is the wise man? Where is the scholar? Where is the philosopher of this age? Has not God made fool-ish the wisdom of the world? For since in the wisdom of God the world through its wisdom did not know him, God was pleased through the foolishness of what was preached to save those who believe. (1 Corinthians 1:20, 21)

And again:

> Do not deceive yourselves. If any one of you thinks he is wise by the standards of this age, he should become

a "fool" so that he may become wise. For the wisdom
of this world is foolishness in God's sight. (1 Corinthians 3:18, 19)

Now we should say immediately that Paul is not saying that
knowledge and education have no value. Paul himself was among
the most highly educated of his time. Paul is speaking instead of
a worldly wisdom which claims to be self-sufficient in itself, quite
apart from God and his revelation. It is a kind of worldly wisdom which leaves God and his revelation out of the picture and
thereby ends up with a completely distorted conception of reality. This can be seen most clearly in the first chapter of Romans
where Paul writes:

For although they knew God, they neither glorified him
as God nor gave thanks to him, but their thinking became futile and their foolish hearts were darkened. Although they claimed to be wise, they became fools....
    Therefore God gave them over in the sinful de-
sires of their hearts to sexual impurity for the degrad-
ing of their bodies with one another. They exchanged
the truth of God for a lie, and worshiped and served
created things rather than the Creator . . . .(Romans
1:21-25)

What is involved here is the way men think, the process of reasoning, thought, and comprehension. Thus "their thinking became futile and their foolish hearts were darkened. Although they
claimed to be wise, they became fools." When the Scripture
speaks of man being foolish in this way, it does not mean he is
only foolish religiously. Rather, it means that he has accepted a
position that is intellectually foolish not only with regard to what
the Bible says, but also to what exists concerning the universe

and its form and what it means to be human. In turning away from God and the truth which he has given, man has thus become *foolishly* foolish in regard to what man is and what the universe is. Man is left with a position with which he cannot live, and he is caught in a multitude of intellectual and personal tensions.

The Scripture tells us how man came into this situation: Because "although they knew God, they neither glorified him as God nor gave thanks to him"; therefore, they became foolish in their reasoning, in their comprehension, in their lives. This passage relates to the original fall, but it does not speak only about the original fall. It speaks of any period when men knew the truth and deliberately turned away from it.

Many periods of history could be described in this way. From the biblical viewpoint there was a time when the ancestors of the people of India knew the truth and turned away, a time when the ancestors of the people of Africa knew the truth and turned away. This is true of people anywhere who now do not know the truth. But if we are looking across the history of the world to see those times when men knew the truth and turned away, let us say emphatically that there is not an exhibition of this anywhere in history so clearly—and in such a short time— as in our own generation. We who live in North America have seen this verse carried out in our generation with desperate force. Men of our time knew the truth and yet turned away—turned away not only from the biblical truth but also turned away from the many blessings this brought in every area of culture, including the balance of form and freedom we once had.

A Post-Christian Culture
Having turned away from the knowledge given by God, the Christian influence on the whole of culture has been lost. In Europe, including England, it took many years—in the United States

only a few decades. In the United States, in the short span from the twenties to the sixties, we have seen a complete shift. Ours is a post-Christian world in which Christianity, not only in the number of Christians but in cultural emphasis and cultural result, is no longer the consensus or ethos of our society.

Do not take this lightly! It is a horrible thing for a man like myself to look back and see my country and my culture go down the drain in my own lifetime. It is a horrible thing that sixty years ago you could move across this country and almost everyone, even non-Christians, would have known what the gospel was. A horrible thing that fifty to sixty years ago our culture was built on the Christian consensus, and now this is no longer the case.

Once again I would refer to Romans 1:21, 22: "although they knew God, they neither glorified him as God nor gave thanks to him, but their thinking became futile and their foolish hearts were darkened. Although they claimed to be wise, they became fools." Verse 18 tells us of the result of turning away from and rebelling against the truth they know: "The wrath of God is being revealed from heaven against all the godlessness and wickedness of men who suppress the truth by their wickedness." Man is justly under the wrath of the God who really exists and who deals with men on the basis of his character; and if the justice of that wrath is obvious concerning any generation it is our own. Wrath may come either in the cause and effect of the turning wheels of history, or in the direct action of God.

There is only one perspective we can have of the post-Christian world of our generation: an understanding that our culture and our country deserves to be under the wrath of God. It will not do to say the United States is God's country in some special way. It will not do to cover up the difference between the consensus today and the Christian consensus that prevailed sixty years ago. The last few generations have trampled upon the truth of the Bible and all that those truths have brought forth.[9]

Ideas and Actions

We have seen then that as Bible-believing Christians we are locked
in a battle in the area of ideas. But in the area of actions there is
a direct parallel. Ideas are never neutral and abstract. Ideas have
consequences in the way we live and act, both in our personal
lives and in the culture as a whole. We can look again to the first
chapter of Romans to see what the consequences of these ideas
are in the form of actions:

> Therefore God gave them over in the sinful desires of
> their hearts to sexual impurity for the degrading of their
> bodies with one another....
>
> Furthermore, since they did not think it worth-
> while to retain the knowledge of God, he gave them
> over to a depraved mind, to do what ought not to be
> done. They have become filled with every kind of
> wickedness, evil, greed and depravity. They are full
> of envy, murder, strife, deceit and malice. They are
> gossips, slanderers, God-haters, insolent, arrogant and
> boastful; they invent ways of doing evil; they disobey
> their parents; they are senseless, faithless, heartless,
> ruthless. Although they know God's righteous decree
> that those who do such things deserve death, they not
> only continue to do these very things but also approve
> of those who practice them. (Romans 1:24, 28-32)

There hardly could be a more fitting description of our own
culture today. Bent on the pursuit of autonomous freedom—freedom from any restraint, and especially from God's truth and moral
absolutes—our culture has set itself on the course of self-de-
struction. Autonomous freedom! How the voices of our day cry
out! I must be free to kill the child in my womb. I must be free
even to kill the newborn child if I don't think he or she measures

up to my standards of "quality life." I must be free to desert my husband or wife, and abandon my children. I must be free to commit shameless acts with those of my own sex. The last verse really is frightening when we think of it in relationship to our culture today: "Although they know God's righteous decree that those who do such things deserve death, they not only continue to do these very things but also approve of those who practice them."

And if this is not enough, I would urge you to read the second chapter of 2 Peter. The whole chapter is as accurate a picture of our culture as can be found anywhere—of the knowledge we once had, of the rejection of the truth, of the moral degeneration, and of the judgment that awaits those who have known the truth and turned from it. Thus Peter concludes the chapter:

> For they mouth empty, boastful words and, by appealing to the lustful desires of sinful human nature, they entice people who are just escaping from those who live in error. They promise them freedom, while they themselves are slaves of depravity—for a man is a slave to whatever has mastered him. If they have escaped the corruption of the world by knowing our Lord and Savior Jesus Christ and are again entangled in it and overcome, they are worse off at the end than they were at the beginning. It would have been better for them not to have known the way of righteousness, than to have known it and then to turn their backs on the sacred commandment that was passed on to them. (2 Peter 2:18-21)

Make no mistake. We as Bible-believing evangelical Christians are locked in a battle. This is not a friendly gentleman's discussion. It is a life and death conflict between the spiritual hosts of wickedness and those who claim the name of Christ. It is a conflict on the level of ideas between two fundamentally opposed views of truth and reality. It is a conflict on the level of actions between a complete moral perversion and chaos and God's absolutes. But do we really believe that we are in a life and death battle? Do we really believe that the part we play in the battle has consequences for whether or not men and women will spend eternity in hell? Or whether or not in this life people will live with meaning or meaninglessness? Or whether or not those who do live will live in a climate of moral perversion and degradation? Sadly, we must say that very few in the evangelical world have acted as if these things are true. Rather than trumpet our accomplishments and revel in our growing numbers, it would be closer to the truth to admit that our response has been a disaster.

The Antithesis of Christian Truth

In thinking back over what I have said to this point, we have seen that the spirit of the age is autonomous freedom—that is, freedom from all restraints and especially rebellion against God's truth and moral absolutes. And we have seen that over the last sixty years the pursuit of autonomous freedom has undercut the Christian ethos that once had a profound influence in shaping our culture. How did this come about? In one sense we may say that it is due to willful rebellion against God's truth and the revelation of his Word. And we would be right in this. But in another sense the changes which have come flow out of the intellectual and religious history of our culture and the Western world. In a number of my books I have dealt at length with the rise of humanism in the Western world and the devastating effect this has had, and I would encourage you to review this.[10] Here, however, I would refer to just one aspect of this—that is, the influence of the Enlightenment, and how this relates specifically to the shift that has taken place in our country over the last sixty years.

At the end of the nineteenth century the ideas of the Enlightenment began to have a significant influence upon Christianity in America. Now it is important to understand what the views of the Enlightenment were, for they have left a radical mark upon religion in America up to this day. The Enlightenment was a movement of thought which began to appear in the mid-seventeenth century and reached its most clear-cut form in eighteenth-century Germany. In general, it was an intellectual movement which emphasized the sufficiency of human reason and skepticism concerning the validity of the traditional authority of the past. It is instructive to note exactly how the Enlightenment is defined in *The Oxford Dictionary of the Christian Church:*

> The Enlightenment combines opposition to all supernatural religion and belief in the all-sufficiency of human reason with an ardent desire to promote the happiness of men in this life .... Most of its representatives ... rejected the Christian dogma and were hostile to Catholicism as well as Protestant orthodoxy, which they regarded as powers of spiritual darkness depriving humanity of the use of its rational faculties. ... Their fundamental belief in the goodness of human nature, which blinded them to the fact of sin, produced an easy optimism and absolute faith of human society once the principles of enlightened reason had been recognized. The spirit of the Enlightenment penetrated deeply into German Protestantism [in the 19th century], where it disintegrated faith in the authority of the Bible and encouraged Biblical criticism on the one hand and an emotional "Pietism" on the other.[11]

This could be summarized in a few words: The central ideas of the Enlightenment stand in complete antithesis to Christian truth. More than this, they are an attack on God himself and his character.

In the late nineteenth century it was these ideas which began to radically transform Christianity in America. This started especially with the acceptance of the "higher critical" methods that had been developed in Germany. Using these methods, the new liberal theologians completely undercut the authority of Scripture. We can be thankful for those who argued strenuously against the new methods and in defense of the full inspiration and inerrancy of Scripture. One would remember especially the great Princeton theologians A. A. Hodge and B. B. Warfield, and later J. Gresham Machen. But in spite of the efforts of these men and scores of other Bible-believing Christian leaders, and in spite of the fact that the vast majority of lay Christians were truly Bible-believing, those holding the liberal ideas of the Enlightenment and the destructive methods of biblical criticism came into power and control in the denominations. By the 1930s liberalism had swept through most of the denominations and the battle was all but lost.

The Turning-Point
Then in the mid 1930s, there occurred an event which I would say marks the turning-point of the century concerning the breakdown of our culture. By 1936 the liberals were so in control of the Northern Presbyterian Church that they were able to defrock Dr. J. Greshem Machen. Machen, as I mentioned, had been a brilliant defender of Bible-believing Christianity, as can be seen, for example, in his book entitled *Christianity and Liberalism*[12] published in 1924. Machen's defrocking and the resulting division of the Northern Presbyterian Church was front-page news in the secular news media in much of the country. (I would just comment that this is something we know nothing about today. In the 1930s religious events were still considered important enough to

be front-page news.) However much conscious forethought this showed on the editors' and broadcasters' part, this was rightfully page-one news, for it marked the culmination of the drift of the Protestant churches from 1900-1936. It was this drift which laid the base for the cultural, social, moral, legal, and governmental changes from that time to the present. Without this drift in the denominations, I am convinced that the changes in our society over the last fifty years would have produced very different results from what we have now. When the Reformation churches shifted, the Reformation consensus was undercut. A good case could be made that the news about Machen was the most significant U.S. news in the first half of the twentieth century. It was the culmination of a long trend toward liberalism within the Presbyterian Church and represented the same trend in most other denominations. Even if we were only interested in sociology, this change in the churches and the resulting shift of our culture to a post-Christian consensus is important to understand if we are to grasp what is happening in the United States today.[13] It is interesting to note that there was a span of approximately eighty years from the time when the higher critical methods originated and became widely accepted in Germany to the disintegration of German culture and the rise of totalitarianism under Hitler.

The New Consensus

Do you understand now what the battle is about in the area of culture and ideas? In the last sixty years the consensus upon which our culture was built has shifted from one that was largely Christian (though we must say immediately it was far from perfect) to a consensus growing out of the Enlightenment: that is, to a consensus that stands in total antithesis to Christian truth at every point —including the denial of the supernatural; belief in the all-sufficiency of human reason; the rejection of the fall; denial of the deity of Christ and his resurrection; belief in the perfectibility of

Man; and the destruction of the Bible. And with this has come a nearly total moral breakdown. There is no way to make a synthesis of these ideas and Christian truth. They stand in total antithesis.

In a number of my other books I have described this new consensus as secular humanism. The Enlightenment world view and the world view of secular humanism really are essentially the same, with the same intellectual heritage. What we have here is a total world view. As I said in *A Christian Manifesto,* the problems we face today have:

> come about due to a shift in world view — that is, through a fundamental change in the overall way people think and view the world and life as a whole. This shift has been *away from* a world view that was at least vaguely Christian in people's memory (even if they were not individually Christian) *toward* something completely different — toward a world view based upon the idea that the final reality is impersonal matter or energy shaped into its present form by impersonal chance.[14]

And if we hold this world view we live in a universe that is ultimately silent, with no meaning and purpose, with no basis for law and morality, with no concept of what it means to be human and of the value of human life. All is relative and arbitrary. And so modern man is left with nothing to fill the void but hedonism or materialism or whatever other "ism" may be blowing in the wind.

Accommodation

And now we must ask where we as evangelicals have been in the battle for truth and morality in our culture. Have we as evangelicals been on the front lines contending for the faith and confronting the moral breakdown over the last forty to sixty years? Have we even been aware that there is a battle going on—not just a heavenly battle, but a life-and-death struggle over what will happen to men and women and children in both this life and the next? If the truth of the Christian faith is in fact *truth,* then it stands in antithesis to the ideas and the immorality of our age, and it must be *practiced* both in teaching and practical action. Truth demands confrontation. It must be loving confrontation, but there must be confrontation nonetheless.

Sadly we must say that this has seldom happened. Most of the evangelical world has not been active in the battle, or even been able to see that we are in a battle. And when it comes to the issues of the day the evangelical world most often has said nothing; or worse has said nothing different from what the world would say.

Here is the great evangelical disaster—the failure of the evangelical world to stand for truth as truth. There is only one word for this—namely *accommodation:* the evangelical church has accommodated to the world spirit of the age. First, there has been accommodation on Scripture, so that many who call themselves evangelicals hold a weakened view of the Bible and no longer affirm the truth of all the Bible teaches—truth not only in religious matters but in the areas of science and history and morality. As part of this, many evangelicals are now accepting the higher critical methods in the study of the Bible. Remember, it was these same methods which destroyed the authority of the Bible for the Protestant church in Germany in the last century, and which have destroyed the Bible for the liberal in our own country from the beginning of this century. And second, there has been accommodation on the issues, with no clear stand being taken even on matters of life and death.

This accommodation has been costly, first in destroying

the power of the Scriptures to confront the spirit of our age; second, in allowing the further slide of our culture. Thus we must say with tears that it is the evangelical accommodation to the world spirit around us, to the wisdom of this age, which removes the evangelical church from standing against the further breakdown of our culture. It is my firm belief that when we stand before Jesus Christ, we will find that it has been the weakness and accommodation of the evangelical group on the issues of the day that has been largely responsible for the loss of the Christian ethos which has taken place in the area of culture in our own country over the last forty to sixty years.

And let us understand that to accommodate to the world spirit about us in our age is nothing less than the most gross form of worldliness in the proper definition of that word. And with this proper definition of worldliness, we must say with tears that, with exceptions, the evangelical church is worldly and not faithful to the living Christ.

What Really Matters?

In concluding this chapter I would ask one final question: What really matters? What is it that matters so much in my life and in your life that it sets the priorities for everything we do? Our Lord Jesus was asked essentially this same question and his reply was:

> "'Love the Lord your God with all your heart and with all your soul and with all your mind.' This is the first and greatest commandment. And the second is like it: 'Love your neighbor as yourself.' All the Law and the Prophets hang on these two commandments." (Matthew 22:37-40)

Here is what really matters—to love the Lord our God, to love his Son, and to know him personally as our Savior. And if we love him, to do the things that please him; simultaneously to show forth his character of holiness and love in our lives; to be faithful to his truth; to walk day by day with the living Christ; to live a life of prayer.

And the other half of what really matters is to love our neighbor as ourselves. The two go together; they cannot be separated. "On these two commandments hang all the Law and the Prophets." *Because* we love the Lord Jesus Christ and know him personally as our Savior *we must,* through God's grace, love our neighbor as ourselves. And if we love our neighbor as Christ would have us love our neighbor, we will certainly want to share the gospel with our neighbor; and beyond this we will want to show forth the law of God in all our relationships with our neighbor.

But it does not stop here. Evangelism is primary, but it is not the end of our work and indeed cannot be separated from the rest of the Christian life.[15] We must acknowledge and then act upon the fact that if Christ is our Savior, he is also our Lord in *all* of life. He is our Lord not just in religious things and not just in cultural things such as the arts and music, but in our intellectual lives, and in business, and in our relation to society, and in our attitude toward the moral breakdown of our culture. Acknowledging Christ's Lordship and placing ourselves under what is taught in the whole Bible includes thinking and acting as citizens in relation to our government and its laws.[16] Making Christ Lord in our lives means taking a stand in very direct and practical ways against the world spirit of our age as it rolls along claiming to be autonomous, crushing all that we cherish in its path.

If we truly love our Lord and if we truly love our neighbor, we will ache with compassion for humanity today in our own country and across the world. We must do all we can to help people see the truth of Christianity and accept Christ as Savior. And we must not allow the Bible to be weakened by any compromise in its authority, no matter how subtle the means. This is especially so when those doing this call themselves "evangelical." But we must stand equally aganist the spirit of our age in the breakdown of morality and the terrible loss of humanness that it has brought. It will mean especially standing for human life and showing by our actions that every life is sacred and worthwhile in itself—not only to us as human beings, but precious also to God. Every person is worth fighting for, regardless of whether he is young or old, sick or well, child or adult, born or unborn, or brown, red, yellow, black, or white.

It is God's life-changing power that is able to touch every individual, who then has the responsibility to touch the world around him with the absolutes found in the Bible. In the end we must realize that the spirit of the age—with all the loss of truth and beauty, and the loss of compassion and humanness that it has brought — is not merely a cultural ill. It is a spiritual ill that the truth given us in the Bible and Christ alone can cure.

PART II:

THE WATERSHED OF THE EVANGELICAL WORLD

CHAPTER 2

Marking the Watershed

A Watershed

Not far from where we live in Switzerland is a high ridge of rock with a valley on both sides. One time I was there when there was snow on the ground along that ridge. The snow was lying there unbroken, a seeming unity. However, that unity was an illusion, for it lay along a great divide; it lay along a watershed. One portion of the snow when it melted would flow into one valley. The snow which lay close beside would flow into another valley when it melted.

Now it just so happens on that particular ridge that the melting snow which flows down one side of that ridge goes down into a valley, into a small river, and then down into the Rhine River. The Rhine then flows on through Germany and the water ends up in the cold waters of the North Sea. The water from the snow that started out so close along that watershed on the other side of the ridge, when this snow melts, drops off sharply down the ridge into the Rhone Valley. This water flows into

Lac Leman—or as it is known in the English-speaking world, Lake Geneva—and then goes down below that into the Rhone River which flows through France and into the warm waters of the Mediterranean.

The snow lies along that watershed, unbroken, as a seeming unity. But when it melts, where it ends in its destinations is literally a thousand miles apart. That is a watershed. That is what a watershed is. A watershed divides. A clear line can be drawn between what seems at first to be the same or at least very close, but in reality ends in very different situations. In a watershed there is a line.

A House Divided

What does this illustration have to do with the evangelical world today? I would suggest that it is a very accurate description of what is happening. Evangelicals today are facing a watershed concerning the nature of biblical inspiration and authority. It is a watershed issue in very much the same sense as described in the illustration. Within evangelicalism there is a growing number who are modifying their views on the inerrancy of the Bible so that the full authority of Scripture is completely undercut. But it is happening in very subtle ways. Like the snow lying side-by-side on the ridge, the new views on biblical authority often seem at first glance not to be so very far from what evangelicals, until just recently, have always believed. But also, like the snow lying side-by-side on the ridge, the new views when followed consistently end up a thousand miles apart.

What may seem like a minor difference at first, in the end makes all the difference in the world. It makes all the difference, as we might expect, in things pertaining to theology, doctrine and spiritual matters, but it also makes all the difference in things pertaining to the daily Christian life and how we as Christians are to relate to the world around us. In other words, *compromis-*

ing the full authority of Scripture eventually affects what it means
to be a Christian theologically and how we live in the full spec-
trum of human life.

There is a sense in which the problem of full biblical authority is fairly recent. Up until the last two hundred years or so
virtually every Christian believed in the complete inerrancy of
the Bible, or in the equivalent of this expressed in similar terms.
This was true both before the Reformation and after. The problem with the pre-Reformation medieval church was not so much
that it did not hold to belief in an inerrant Bible as that it allowed
the whole range of nonbiblical theological ideas and superstitions to grow up within the church. These ideas were then placed
alongside of the Bible and even over the Bible, so that the
Bible's authority and teaching were subordinated to nonbiblical
teachings. This resulted in the abuses which led to the Reformation. But note that the problem was not that the pre-Reformation church did not *believe* in the inerrancy of Scripture; the
problem was that it did not *practice* the inerrancy of Scripture,
because it subordinated the Bible to its fallible teachings.

Thus it is important to note that, up until recent times, 1)
belief in the inerrancy of Scripture (even when it was not practiced fully) and 2) claiming to be a Christian were seen as two
things which necessarily went together. If you were a Christian,
you also trusted in the complete reliability of God's written Word,
the Bible. If you did not believe the Bible, you did not claim to
be a Christian. But no one, until the past two hundred years or
so, tried to say, "I am a Christian, but at the same time I believe
the Bible to be full of errors." As incredible as this would have
seemed to Christians in the past, and as incredible as this may
seem to Bible-believing Christians today, this is what is now
happening within the evangelical world.

This problem which started some two hundred years ago
has within the past two decades come to the forefront among

evangelicals. It is a problem which I (and others) began to address publicly in the mid-sixties, again in the seventies and repeatedly in the eighties. We can be thankful for the many who have taken a strong stand on this; but we must also say, sadly, that the problem continues and is growing. Evangelicalism is divided, deeply divided. And it will not be helpful or truthful for anyone to deny this. It is something that will not simply go away, and it cannot be swept under the rug. What follows in this chapter grows out of the study, thinking, and prayer, often with tears, which I have done concerning this watershed issue during my whole life as a Christian, but especially as I have dealt with this in my speaking and writing during the past two decades. The following, then, is a restatement on further development as a unified whole of my work in this area.

The Ground Cut out from Under

There are two reasons in our day for holding to a strong uncompromising view of Scripture. First and foremost, this is the only way to be faithful to what the Bible teaches about itself, to what Christ teaches about Scripture, and to what the church has consistently held through the ages. This should be reason enough in itself. But today there is a second reason why we should hold to a strong, uncompromising view of Scripture. There are hard days ahead of us—for ourselves and for our spiritual and physical children. And without a strong view of Scripture as a foundation, we will not be ready for the hard days to come. Unless the Bible is without error, not only when it speaks of salvation matters, but also when it speaks of history and the cosmos, we have no foundation for answering questions concerning the existence of the universe and its form and the uniqueness of man. Nor do we have any moral absolutes, or certainty of salvation, and the next generation of Christians will have nothing on which to stand. Our spiritual and physical children will be left with the ground cut out from under them, with no foundation upon which to build their faith or their lives.

Christianity is no longer providing the consensus for our society. And Christianity is no longer providing the consensus upon which our law is based. That is not to say that the United States ever was a "Christian nation" in the sense that all or most of our citizens were Christians, nor in the sense that the nation, its laws, and social life were ever a full and complete expression of Christian truth. There is no golden age in the past which we can idealize—whether it is early America, the Reformation, or the early church. But until recent decades something did exist which can rightly be called a Christian consensus or ethos which gave a distinctive shape to Western society and to the United States in a definite way. Now that consensus is all but gone, and the freedoms that it brought are being destroyed before our eyes. We are at a time when humanism is coming to its natural conclusion in morals, in values, and in law. All that society has today are relativistic values based upon statistical averages, or the arbitrary decisions of those who hold legal and political power.

Freedom with Form or Chaos
The Reformation with its emphasis upon the Bible, in all that it teaches, as being the revelation of God, provided a freedom in society and yet a form in society as well. Thus, there were freedoms in the Reformation countries (such as the world had never known before) without those freedoms leading to chaos—because both laws and morals were surrounded by a consensus resting upon what the Bible taught. That situation is now finished, and we cannot understand society today for ourselves or our spiritual and physical children unless we understand in reality what has happened. In retrospect we can see that ever since the 1930s in the United States, the Christian consensus has been an increasingly minority view and no longer provides a consensus for

society in morals or law. We who are Bible-believing Christians no longer represent the prevailing legal and moral outlook of our society, and no longer have the major influence in shaping this.

The primary emphasis of biblical Christianity is the teaching that the infinite-personal God is the final reality, the Creator of all else, and that an individual can come openly to the holy God upon the basis of the finished work of Christ and that alone. Nothing needs to be added to Christ's finished work, and nothing *can* be added to Christ's finished work. But at the same time where Christianity provides the consensus, as it did in the Reformation countries (and did in the United States up to a relatively few years ago), Christianity also brings with it many secondary blessings. One of these has been titanic freedoms, yet without those freedoms leading to chaos, because the Bible's *absolutes* provide a consensus within which freedom can operate. But once the Christian consensus has been removed, as it has been today, then the very freedoms which have come out of the Reformation become a destructive force leading to chaos in society. This is why we see the breakdown of morality everywhere in our society today—the complete devaluation of human life, a total moral relativism, and a thoroughgoing hedonism.

Relativism or God's Absolutes

In such a setting, we who are Bible-believing Christians, or our children, face days of decision ahead. Soft days for evangelical Christians are past, and only a strong view of Scripture is sufficient to withstand the pressure of an all-pervasive culture built upon relativism and relativistic thinking. We must remember that it was a strong view of the absolutes which the infinite-personal God gave to the early church in the Old Testament, in the revelation of Christ through the Incarnation, and in the then growing New Testament—absolutes which enabled the early church to withstand the pressure of the Roman Empire. Without a strong commitment to God's absolutes, the early church could never have remained faithful in the face of the constant Roman harassment and persecution. And our situation today is remarkably similar as our own legal, moral, and social structure is based on an increasingly anti-Christian, secularist consensus.

But what is happening in evangelicalism today? Is there the same commitment to God's absolutes which the early church had? Sadly we must say that this commitment is not there. Although growing in numbers as far as name is concerned, throughout the world and the United States, evangelicalism is not unitedly standing for a strong view of Scripture. But we must say if evangelicals are to be evangelicals, we must not compromise our view of Scripture. There is no use of evangelicalism seeming to get larger and larger, if at the same time appreciable parts of evangelicalism are getting soft concerning the Scriptures.

We must say with sadness that in some places seminaries, institutions, and individuals who are known as evangelicals no longer hold to a full view of Scripture. The issue is clear. Is the Bible true truth and infallible wherever it speaks, including where it touches history and the cosmos, or is it only in some sense revelational where it touches religious subjects? That is the issue.

The New Neo-Orthodoxy

There is only one way to describe those who no longer hold to a full view of Scripture. Although many of these would like to retain the evangelical name for themselves, the only accurate way to describe this view is that it is a form of neo-orthodox existential theology. The heart of neo-orthodox existential theology is that the Bible gives us a quarry out of which to have religious experience, but that the Bible contains mistakes where it touches that which is verifiable—namely history and science. But unhappily we must say that in some circles this concept now has come into some of that which is called evangelicalism. In short, in these circles the neo-orthodox existential theology is being taught under the name of evangelicalism.

The issue is whether the Bible gives propositional truth (that is, truth which may be stated in propositions) where it touches history and the cosmos, and this all the way back to pre-Abrahamic history, all the way back to the first eleven chapters of Genesis; or whether instead of that, it is only meaningful where it touches that which is considered religious. T. H. Huxley, the biologist friend of Darwin, the grandfather of Aldous and Julian Huxley, wrote in 1890 that he visualized the day not far hence in which faith would be separated from all fact, and especially all pre-Abrahamic history, and that faith would then go on triumphant forever. This is an amazing statement for 1890, before the birth of existential philosophy or existential theology. Huxley indeed foresaw something clearly. I am sure that he and his friends considered this some kind of a joke, because they would have understood well that if faith is separated from fact and specifically pre-Abrahamic space-time history, it is only another form of what we today call a trip.

But unhappily, it is not only the avowedly neo-orthodox existential theologians who now hold that which T. H. Huxley foresaw, but some who call themselves evangelicals as well. This may come from the theological side in saying that not all the Bible is revelational. Or it may come from the scientific side in saying that the Bible teaches little or nothing when it speaks of the cosmos. Or it may come from the cultural side in saying that the moral teachings of the Bible were merely expressions of the culturally determined and relative situation in which the Bible was written and therefore not authoritative today.

Martin Luther said, "If I profess with the loudest voice and clearest exposition every portion of the truth of God except precisely that little point which the world and the devil are at the moment attacking, I am not confessing Christ, however boldly I may be professing Christ. Where the battle rages, there the loyalty of the soldier is proved and to be steady on all the battle front besides, is mere flight and disgrace if he flinches at that point."

Marking a Line
In our day that point is the question of Scripture. Holding to a strong view of Scripture or not holding to it is the watershed of the evangelical world.

The first direction in which we must face is to say most lovingly but clearly: evangelicalism is not consistently evangelical *unless there is a line drawn* between those who take a full view of Scripture and those who do not.

What is often forgotten is that where there is a watershed there is a line which can be observed and marked. If one had the responsibility in Switzerland, for example, for the development of hydroelectric power from the flow of water, one would have a great responsibility to determine the topography of the country and then mark where the line would fall, and where the water would divide and flow. In the watershed of the evangelical world, what does marking such a line mean? It means lovingly marking visibly where that line falls, lovingly showing that some are on the other side of the line, and making clear to everyone on both sides of the line what the consequences of this are.

In making visible where the line falls, we must understand what is really happening. With the denial of the full authority of Scripture, a significant section of what is called evangelicalism has allowed itself to be infiltrated by the general world view or viewpoint of our day. This infiltration *is really a variant of what had dominated liberal theological circles under the name of neo-orthodoxy.*

An Inner Feeling or Objective Truth
It is surprising to see how clearly the liberal, neo-orthodox way of thinking is reflected in the new weakened evangelical

view. For example, some time ago I was on Milt Rosenberg's radio show "Extension 720" in Chicago (WGN) along with a young liberal pastor who graduated from a very well-known liberal theological seminary. The program was set up as a three-way discussion between myself, the liberal pastor, and Rosenberg, who does not consider himself to be a religious person. Rosenberg is a clever master of discussion. And with *A Christian Manifesto* and the question of abortion as the discussion points, he kept digging deeper and deeper into the difference between the young liberal pastor and myself. The young liberal pastor brought up Karl Barth, Niebuhr, and Tillich, and we discussed them. But it became very clear in that three-way discussion that the young liberal pastor never could appeal to the Bible without qualifications. And then the young liberal pastor said, "But I appeal to Jesus." My reply on the radio was that in view of his view of the Bible, he could not really be sure that Jesus lived. His answer was that he had an inner feeling, an inner response, that told him that Jesus had existed.

The intriguing thing to me was that one of the leading men of the weakened view of the Bible who is called an evangelical, and who certainly does love the Lord, in a long and strenuous but pleasant discussion in my home a few years ago, when pressed backwards as to how he was certain concerning the resurrection of Jesus Christ, used almost the same words. He said he was sure of the resurrection of Jesus Christ because of the inward witness. They both answered finally in the same way.

My point is that a significant and influential section of what is called evangelicalism has become infiltrated by a point of view which is directly related to the view that had dominated liberal theological circles under the name of neo-orthodoxy. To me, this was curious at the time when I saw it happening a certain number of years ago because where this ends had already been demonstrated by the Neibuhr-Tillich-"God-is-dead" syndrome. Neo-orthodoxy leads to a dead end with a dead God, as has already been demonstrated by the theology of the sixties. And is it not curious that some evangelicals are just now picking this up as if it were the thing we should hold if we are to be "with it" today? But equally significant, note that the liberal pastor and the leader with the weakened view of Scripture who calls himself an evangelical both end up in the same place—with no other final plea than "an inner witness." They have no final, objective authority.

This points up just how encompassing the infiltration is. Namely, just as the neo-orthodox roots are only a theological expression of the surrounding world view and methodology of existentialism, so what is being put forth as a new view of Scripture in evangelicalism is also an infiltration of the general world view and methodology of existentialism. By placing a radical emphasis on subjective human experience, existentialism undercuts the objective side of existence. For the existentialist it is an illusion to think that we can know anything truly, that there is such a thing as certain objective truth or moral absolutes. All we have is subjective experience, with no final basis for right or wrong or truth or beauty. This existential world view dominates philosophy, and much of art and the general culture such as the novel, poetry, and the cinema. And although this is apparent in the thinking in academic and philosophical circles, it is equally pervasive in popular culture. It is impossible to turn on the TV, or read the newspaper, or leaf through a popular magazine without being bombarded with the philosophy of moral relativism, subjective experience, and the denial of objective truth. In the new view of Scripture among evangelicals we find the same thing—namely, that the Bible is not objective truth; that in the area of what is verifiable it has many mistakes in it; that where it touches on history and the cosmos it cannot be trusted; and that even what it teaches concerning morality is culturally conditioned and cannot be accepted in an absolute sense. But nevertheless this new weakened view stresses that "a religious word" somehow breaks through from the Bible—which finally ends in some expression such as "an inner feeling," "an inner response," or "an inner witness."

A Divided Bible

The following two quotations are clear examples of this. They come from men widely separated geographically across the world, both of whom are in evangelical circles, but who advocate the idea that in the area where reason operates the Bible contains mistakes. The first writes:

> But there are some today who regard the Bible's plen-
> ary and verbal inspiration as insuring its inerrancy not
> only in its declared intention to recount and interpret
> God's mighty redemptive acts, but also in any and in
> all of its incidental statements or aspects of statements
> that have to do with such nonrevelational matters as
> geology, meteorology, cosmology, botany, astron-
> omy, geography, etc.

In other words, the Bible is divided into halves. To someone like myself this is all very familiar—in the writings of Jean-Paul Sartre, of Albert Camus, of Martin Heidegger, of Karl Jaspers, and in the case of thousands of modern people who have accepted the existential methodology. This quotation is saying the same thing they would say, but specifically relating this existential meth-odology to the Bible.

In a similar quote another evangelical leader in a country far from the United States writes:

> More problematic in my estimation is the fundamen-

talist extension of the principle of noncontradictory
Scriptures to include the historic, geographic, statistical and other biblical statements, which do not touch
in every case on the question of salvation and which
do belong to the human element of Scripture.

Both of these statements do the same thing. They make a
dichotomy; they make a division. They say that there are mistakes in the Bible but nevertheless we are to keep hold of the
meaning system, the value system, and the religious things. This
then is the form in which the existential methodology has come
into evangelical circles. In the end it cuts the truth of the Scriptures off from the objective world and replaces it with the subjective experience of an "inner witness." It reminds us in particular of the secular existential philosopher Karl Jaspers' term
"the final experience," and any number of other terms which are
some form of the concept of final authority being an inner witness. In the neo-orthodox form, the secular existential form, and
this new evangelical form, truth is left finally as only subjective.

All this stands in sharp contrast to the historic view presented by Christ himself and the historic view of the Scripture in
the Christian church, which is the Bible being objective, absolute truth. Of course we all know that there are subjective ele-
ments involved in our personal reading of the Bible and in the
church's reading of the Bible. But nevertheless, the Bible *is* objective, absolute truth in all the areas it touches upon. And therefore we know that Christ lived, and that Christ was raised from
the dead, and all the rest, not because of some subjective inner
experience, but because the Bible stands as an objective, absolute authority. This is the way we know. I do not downplay the
experience that rests upon this objective reality, but this is the
way we know—upon the basis that the Bible is objective, absolute truth.

Or to say it another way: the culture is to be constantly judged by the Bible, rather than the Bible being bent to conform to the surrounding culture. The early church did this in regard to the Roman-Greek culture of its day. The Reformation did this in its day in relation to the culture coming at the end of the Middle Ages. And we must never forget that all the great revivalists did this concerning the surrounding culture of their day. And the Christian church did this at every one of its great points of history.

The New Loophole

But to complicate things further, there are those within evangelicalism who are quite happy to use the words "infallibility," "inerrancy," and "without error," but upon careful analysis they really mean something quite different from what these words have meant to the church historically. This problem can be seen in what has happened to the statement on Scripture in the Lausanne Covenant of 1974. The statement reads:

> We affirm the divine inspiration, truthfulness and authority of both Old and New Testament Scriptures in their entirety as the only written Word of God, without error in all that it affirms, and the only infallible rule of faith and practice.

Upon first reading, this seems to make a strong statement in support of the full authority of the Bible. But a problem has come up concerning the phrase "in all that it affirms." For many this is being used as a loophole. I ought to say that this little phrase was not a part of my own contribution to the Lausanne Congress. I did not know that this phrase was going to be included in the Covenant until I saw it in printed form, and I was not completely happy with it. Nevertheless, it is a proper statement if the words are dealt with fairly. We do not, of course, want to say that the

Bible is without error in things it does *not* affirm. One of the clearest examples is where the Bible says, "The fool has said in his heart, 'There is no God.'" The Bible does not teach that "there is no God." This is not something that the Bible affirms, even though it makes this statement. Furthermore, we are not saying the Bible is without error in all *the projections* which people have made on the basis of the Bible. So that statement, as it appeared in the Lausanne Covenant, is a perfectly proper statement in itself.

However, as soon as I saw it in printed form I knew it was going to be abused. Unhappily, this statement, "in all that it affirms," has indeed been made a loophole by many. How has it been made a loophole? It has been made a loophole through the existential methodology which would say that the Bible affirms the value system and certain religious things set forth in the Bible. But on the basis of the existential methodology, these men and women say in the back of their minds, even as they sign the Covenant, "But the Bible does not affirm without error that which it teaches in the area of history and the cosmos."

Because of the widely accepted existential methodology in certain parts of the evangelical community, the old words *infallibility, inerrancy* and *without error* are meaningless today unless some phrase is added such as: the Bible is without error not only when it speaks of values, the meaning system, and religious things, but it is also without error when it speaks of history and the cosmos. If some such phrase is not added, these words today are meaningless. It should be especially noted that the word *infallibility* is used today by men who do not apply it to the whole of Scripture, but only to the meaning system, to the value system, and certain religious things, leaving out anyplace where the Bible speaks of history and the things which would interest science.

In Spite of All the Mistakes

Just a few months ago a very clear example of this was brought to my attention. Today we find that the same view of Scripture which is held by the modern liberal theologian is being taught in seminaries which call themselves evangelical. This view follows the existential methodology of secular thinkers which says that the Bible has mistakes but that it is to be believed somehow or other anyway. For example I recently received a letter from a very able thinker in Great Britain, in which he wrote:

> There are many problems facing evangelicals today not the least of which is the neo-orthodoxy in relation to Scripture. I am studying at Tyndale House [a study center in Cambridge, England] for a few days. And down the corridor from me is a very amiable professor, from a prominent seminary in California which calls itself evangelical, who calls himself an "open evangelical." He has stated publicly in theological debate that he believes the Bible "despite all the mistakes in it."

This Christian leader in England who wrote this letter to me is quite right in calling this neo-orthodoxy under the name of evangelical. Isn't it curious that evangelicals have picked this up now as that which is progressive, just at a time when the liberals have found that neo-orthodoxy led to the "God is dead" theology? And when it was clear a few years ago that this seminary and others were simply presenting a form of neo-orthodoxy in regard to Scripture under the evangelical name, did the evangelical leadership quickly draw a line? Was there a rush of the evangelical leadership to the cause of defending the Scriptures and the faith? Sadly we must say no. Except for a few lone voices there was a great, vast silence.[1]

Cultural Infiltration

Those weakening the Bible in the area of history and where it touches the cosmos do so by saying these things in the Bible are *culturally oriented*. That is, in places where the Bible speaks of history and the cosmos, it only shows forth views held by the culture in the day in which that portion of the Bible was written. For example, when Genesis and Paul affirm, as they clearly do, that Eve came from Adam, this is said to be only borrowed from the general cultural views of the day in which these books were written. Thus not just the first eleven chapters of Genesis, but the New Testament is seen to be relative instead of absolute.

But let us realize that one cannot begin such a process without going still further. These things have gone further among some who still call themselves evangelicals. They have been still trying to hold on to the value system, the meaning system, and the religious things given in the Bible; but for them the Bible is only culturally oriented where it speaks of history and the cosmos. In more recent years an extension has come to this. Now certain moral absolutes in the area of personal relationships given in the Bible are also said to be culturally oriented. I would mention two examples, although many others could be given. First, there is easy divorce and remarriage. What the Bible clearly teaches about the limitations placed upon divorce and remarriage is now put by some evangelicals in the area of cultural orientation. They say these were just the ideas of that moment when the New Testament was written. What the Bible teaches on these matters is to them only one more culturally oriented thing, and that is all. There are members, elders, and ministers in churches known as evangelical who no longer feel bound by what the Scripture affirms concerning this matter. They say that what the Bible teaches in this area is culturally oriented and is not to be taken as an absolute.

As a second example, we find the same thing happening

in the area of the clear biblical teaching regarding order in the home and the church. The commands in regard to this order are now also considered culturally oriented by some speakers and writers under the name of evangelical.

In other words, in the last few years the situation has moved from hanging on to the value system, the meaning system, and the religious things while saying that what the Bible affirms in regard to history and the cosmos is culturally oriented to the further step of still trying to hold on to the value system, the meaning system, and religious things, but now lumping these moral commands along with the things of history and the cosmos as culturally oriented. There is no end to this. The Bible is made to say only that which echoes the surrounding culture at *our* moment of history. *The Bible is bent to the culture instead of the Bible judging our society and culture.*

Once men and women begin to go down the path of the existential methodology under the name of evangelicalism, the Bible is no longer the Word of God without error — each part may be eaten away step by step. When men and women come to this place, what then has the Bible become? It has become what the liberal theologians said it was back in the days of the twenties and thirties. We are back in the days of a scholar like J. Gresham Machen, who pointed out that the foundation upon which Christianity rests was being destroyed. What is that foundation? It is that the infinite-personal God who exists has not been silent, but has spoken propositional truth in *all* that the Bible teaches— including what it teaches concerning history, concerning the cosmos, and in moral absolutes as well as what it teaches concerning religious subjects.

Notice though what the primary problem was, and is: infiltration by a form of the world view which surrounds us, rather than the Bible being the unmovable base for judging the ever-shifting fallen culture. As evangelicals, we need to stand at the point of the call *not* to be infiltrated by this ever-shifting fallen culture which surrounds us, but rather judging that culture upon the basis of the Bible.

What Difference Does It Make?

Does inerrancy make a difference? Overwhelmingly; the difference is that with the Bible being what it is, God's Word and so absolute, God's objective truth, we do not need to be, *and we should not be*, caught in the ever-changing fallen cultures which surround us. Those who do not hold the inerrancy of Scripture do not have this high privilege. To some extent, they are at the mercy of the fallen, changing culture. And Scripture is thus bent to conform to the changing world spirit of the day, and they therefore have no solid authority upon which to judge and to resist the views and values of that changing, shifting world spirit.

We, however, must be careful before the Lord. If we say we believe the Bible to be the inerrant and authoritative "Thus saith the Lord," we do not face the howling winds of change which surround us with confusion and terror. And yet, the other side of the coin is that if this *is* the "Thus saith the Lord," we must live under it. And without that, we don't understand what we have said when we say we stand for an inerrant Scripture.

I would ask again, Does inerrancy really make a difference—in the way we live our lives across the whole spectrum of human existence? Sadly we must say that we evangelicals who truly hold to the full authority of Scripture have not always done well in this respect. I have said that inerrancy is the watershed of the evangelical world. But it is not just a theological debating point. *It is the obeying of the Scripture which is the watershed! It is believing and applying it to our lives* which demonstrate whether we in fact believe it.

Hedonism

We live in a society today where all things are relative and the final value is whatever makes the individual or society "happy" or feel good at the moment. This is not just the hedonistic young person doing what feels good; it is society as a whole. This has many facets, but one is the breakdown of all stability in society. Nothing is fixed, there are no final standards; only what makes one "happy" is dominant. This is even true with regard to human life. The January 11, 1982, issue of *Newsweek* had a cover story of about five or six pages which showed conclusively that human life begins at conception. All students of biology should have known this all along. Then one turns the page, and the next article is entitled "But Is It a Person?" The conclusion of that page is, "The problem is not determining when actual human life begins, but when the value of that life begins to outweigh other considerations, such as the health or even the happiness of the mother." The terrifying phrase is, "or even the happiness." Thus, even acknowledged human life can be and is ended for the sake of someone else's happiness.

With no set values, all that matters is my or society's happiness at the moment. I must say I cannot understand why even the liberal lawyers of the American Civil Liberties Union are not terrified at that point.

And, of course, it is increasingly accepted that if a newborn baby is going to make the family or society unhappy, it too should be allowed to die. All you have to do is look at your television programs and this comes across increasingly like a flood. It is upon such a view that Stalin and Mao allowed (and I'm using a very gentle word when I say "allowed") millions to die for what they considered the happiness of society. This then is the terror that surrounds the church today. The individual's or society's happiness takes supreme preference even over human life.

Now let us realize that we are in as much danger of being infiltrated by the surrounding amoral thought-forms of our culture as we are in danger of being infiltrated by the existential thought-forms. Why? Because we are surrounded by a society with no fixed standards and "no-fault" everything. Each thing is psychologically pushed away or explained away so that there is no right or wrong. And, as with the "happiness" of the mother taking precedence over human life, so anything which interferes with the "happiness" of the individual or society is dispensed with.

Bending the Bible

It is obeying the Scriptures which really is the watershed. We can say the Bible is without mistake and still destroy it if we bend the Scriptures by our lives to fit this culture instead of judging the culture by Scripture. And today we see this happening more and more as in the case of easy divorce and remarriage. The no-fault divorce laws in many of our states are not really based upon humanitarianism or kindness. They are based on the view that there is no right and wrong. And thus all is relative, which means that society and the individual act on what seems to give them happiness for the moment.

Do we not have to agree that even much of the evangelical church, which claims to believe that the Bible is without error, has bent Scripture at the point of divorce to conform to the culture rather than the Scripture judging the present viewpoints of the fallen culture? Do we not have to agree that in the area of divorce and remarriage there has been a lack of biblical teaching and discipline even among evangelicals? When I, contrary to Scripture, claim the right to attack the family—not the family in general, but to attack and break up my own family—is it not the same as a mother claiming the right to kill her own baby for her "happiness"? I find it hard to say, but here is an infiltration of the surrounding society that is as destructive to Scripture as is a theological attack upon Scripture. Both are a tragedy. Both bend the Scripture to conform to the surrounding culture.

The Mark of Our Age

What is the use of evangelicalism seeming to get larger and larger if sufficient numbers of those under the name evangelical no longer hold to that which makes evangelicalism evangelical? If this continues, we are not faithful to what the Bible claims for itself, and we are not faithful to what Jesus Christ claims for the Scriptures. But also—let us not ever forget—if this continues, we and our children will not be ready for difficult days ahead.

Furthermore, if we acquiesce, we will no longer be the redeeming salt for our culture—a culture which is committed to the concept that both morals and laws are only a matter of cultural orientation, of statistical averages. That is the hallmark—the mark of our age. And if we are marked with the same mark, how can we be the redeeming salt to this broken, fragmented generation in which we live?

Here then is the watershed of the evangelical world. We must say most lovingly but clearly: evangelicalism is not consistently evangelical unless there is a line drawn between those who take a full view of Scripture and those who do not. But remember that we are not just talking about an abstract theological doctrine. It makes little difference in the end if Scripture is compromised by theological infiltration or by infiltration from the surrounding culture. It is the obeying of Scripture which is the watershed—obeying the Bible equally in doctrine and in the way we live in the full spectrum of life.

Confrontation

But if we truly believe this, then something must be considered. *Truth carries with it confrontation.* Truth *demands* confrontation; loving confrontation, but confrontation nevertheless. If our reflex action is always accommodation regardless of the centrality of the truth involved, there is something wrong. Just as what we may call holiness without love is not God's kind of holiness, so also what we may call love without holiness, including when necessary confrontation, is not God's kind of love. God is holy, and God is love.

We must, with prayer, say no to the theological attack upon Scripture. We must say no to this, clearly and lovingly, with strength. And we must say no to the attack upon Scripture which comes from our being infiltrated in our lives by the current world view of no-fault in moral issues. We must say no to these things equally.

The world of our day has no fixed values and standards, and therefore what people conceive as their personal or society's happiness covers everything. We are not in that position. We have the inerrant Scripture. Looking to Christ for strength against tremendous pressure because our whole culture is against us at this point, we must reject the infiltration in theology and in life equally. We both must affirm the inerrancy of Scripture and then live under it in our personal lives and in society.

God's Word will never pass away, but looking back to the Old Testament and since the time of Christ, with tears we must say that because of lack of fortitude and faithfulness on the part of God's people, God's Word has many times been allowed to be bent, to conform to the surrounding, passing, changing culture of that moment rather than to stand as the inerrant Word of God judging the form of the world spirit and the surrounding culture of that moment. In the name of the Lord Jesus Christ, may our children and grandchildren not say that such can be said about us.

CHAPTER 3

The Practice of Truth

When the Scriptures are being destroyed by theological infiltration and compromise, and equally by cultural infiltration and compromise, will we have the courage as Bible-believing Christians to mark the watershed? Will we have the courage to draw a line, and to do it publicly, between those who take a full view of Scripture and those who have been infiltrated theologically and culturally? If we do not have the courage, we will cut the ground out from under the feet of our children, and we will destroy any hope of being the redeeming salt and light of our dying culture.

We cannot wait for others to draw the line. *We* must draw the line. It will not be easy, and for many it may be costly. It certainly will not be popular. But if we truly believe in the infinite-personal God—the God of holiness and love—if we truly love the Lord and his Word and his church, we have no other choice.

A New "Fundamentalist Legalism"

When Dr. C. Everett Koop, my son Franky, and I were in the midst of seminars for the film *Whatever Happened to the Human Race?* an interesting thing happened. One of us received a letter from a prominent evangelical leader. He holds a good view theologically concerning Scripture, and I would also say that I like him. In his letter, however, he said, "I see the emergence of a new sort of fundamentalist legalism." He went on to explain what he meant like this: "That was the case in the thrust concerning false evangelicals in the inerrancy issue, and is also the case on the part of some who are now saying that the evangelical cause is betrayed by any who allow any exceptions of any sort in government funding to abortion." This needs some clarification. Basically he is saying that those who believe that we must hold to the inerrancy of Scripture in order to be truly evangelical, and those who also take a strong stand against abortion, are expressing a "new sort of fundamentalist legalism."

In one sense this evangelical leader is quite right. A high view of Scripture and a high view of life go hand-in-hand. You cannot be faithful to what the Bible teaches about the value of human life and be in favor of abortion. But the opposite is also true. Theological infiltration in the form of a low view of Scripture and cultural infiltration in the form of the devaluation of human life likewise go hand-in-hand. He correctly linked the two issues together.

But the term "fundamentalist legalism" presents a problem. Is this what we mean when we speak of drawing the line? Is that what we mean by being faithful to the love and holiness of God?

If what is involved is the heartless, loveless, "fundamentalist legalism" some of us have known so well in the past, of course we do not want it, and we reject it in the name of Christ. The love of God and the holiness of God must always be evident simultaneously. And if anyone has wandered off and returns, the attitude should not be one of pride that we have been right, but rather joy and the playing of songs, happy music, joyous music, singing of joyous songs, and I would add, even dancing in the streets because, and if, there has been a true return.

Again, if the term "fundamentalist legalism" means the down-playing of the humanities, as unhappily has so often been the case, the failure to know that the intellect is important, that human creativity by Christians and non-Christians is worth study; if it means the down-playing of the scholarly; if it means the down-playing of the Lordship of Christ in all of life—then my work of some forty years and all my books and films speak of my total rejection of this.

Again, if the term "fundamentalist legalism" means a confusion of primary and secondary points of doctrine and life, that too should be rejected.

Love and Holiness

But when we have said all of this, when we come to the central things of doctrine and to the central things of life itself, then something must be profoundly considered. As I mentioned at the close of the last chapter, truth carries with it confrontation—loving confrontation, but confrontation nonetheless. And if our reflex action is always accommodation regardless of the centrality of the truth involved, then something is profoundly wrong. If we use the word *love* as our excuse for avoiding confrontation when it is necessary, then we have denied the holiness of God and failed to be faithful to him and his true character. In reality we have denied God himself.

It is hard to imagine how far things have gone in just a few years. Something is profoundly wrong when a Bible teacher at a prominent evangelical college teaches that one of the Gospel writers made up some of the stories about the birth of Jesus, and that some of the things which Jesus said as recorded in the Gospels really were not said by Jesus at all, but were made up by other people later. Something is profoundly wrong when many evangelical college and seminary professors now use higher-critical methods to study the Scripture, when it was these same methods which began eighty to one hundred years ago to destroy the Scriptures for the liberal church in the United States. Something is profoundly wrong when the chairman of the philosophy and ethics department at a prominent Christian college holds a proabortion position. Something is profoundly wrong when a leading evangelical changes his position on the full authority of Scripture, endorses the neo-orthodox existential method, and ridicules those who uphold the full authority of Scripture by calling them "Fundamentalist obscurantists."[1]

How must we respond to this—when it is really the gospel itself that is at stake? And more than this, when the future of our culture and the lives of millions are being destroyed?

To be really Bible-believing Christians we need to practice, *simultaneously*, at each step of the way, two biblical principles. One principle is that of the purity of the visible church. Scripture commands that we must do more than just talk about the purity of the visible church; we must actually practice it, even when it is costly.

The second principle is that of an observable love among all true Christians. In the flesh we can stress purity without love, or we can stress love without purity; we cannot stress both simultaneously. To do so we must look moment by moment to the work of Christ and of the Holy Spirit. Without that, a stress on purity becomes hard, proud, and legalistic; likewise, without it a stress on love becomes sheer compromise. Spirituality begins to have real meaning in our lives as we begin to exhibit simultaneously the holiness of God and the love of God. We never do this perfectly, but we must look to the living Christ to help us do it truly. Without this simultaneous exhibition our marvelous God and Lord is not set forth. It is rather a caricature of him that is shown, and he is dishonored.

What Was at Stake?

This is the basis for how we need to respond today. But if we really want to know how these principles apply in the present religious situation, we need to understand what happened in the early decades of this century. We touched on this briefly in Chapter 1, but now we need to look at this much more carefully. During this time a whole course of events took place which left their mark on the church right up to our present day, and they surely will for generations to come. This was the time when the denominations in the United States were in the midst of what often is called the modernist/fundamentalist conflict. But I hesitate to even use this term because most people have a very mistaken understanding of this, especially with the total and deliberate distortion of the word *fundamentalist*.

At the end of the nineteenth and the beginning of the twentieth century, the ideas of liberal German theology came sweeping into this country. These ideas grew out of the German and Western European philosophy current at the time, which basically was an attempt to synthesize the idea of the Enlightenment with theology and thereby to arrive at a "modern" approach to religion in contrast to the "unscientific superstitions" of the past. But there is a problem here: the primary themes of the Enlightenment, as we have seen in Chapter 1, are the complete antithesis to Christian truth. The Enlightenment was founded on the opposition to the supernatural and upon belief in the all-sufficiency in human reason. It held to the fundamental goodness of human nature and believed in the perfectibility of human society. By the time these ideas reached the United States in the late 1800s, they had already penetrated deeply into German Protestantism, disintegrating faith in the Bible through the methods of "higher criticism."[2] Later these ideas entered into portions of the Roman Catholic Church as well.

In the early years of this century, this new liberal theology was coming into the United States like a flood. Most of the large Protestant denominations were being knocked down like a row of tenpins, one after the other, being taken over by liberal theology. But what was really at stake? It was the gospel itself. We are not talking about minor variations in the interpretation of secondary doctrines. We are not talking about denominational differences. The things being denied by the liberals were at the heart of the Christian faith—the authority of the Bible, the deity of Christ, the meaning of salvation. Harry Emerson Fosdick, pastor of the First Presbyterian Church of New York and one of the most influential spokesmen of modernism, was a clear example. In his famous sermon, "Shall the Fundamentalists Win?" given in 1922, he explained what the liberal means by the return of Christ. The liberals, Fosdick preached,

> say "Christ is coming!" They say it with all their hearts; but they are *not thinking of an external arrival on the clouds*. They have *assimilated as part of divine revelation* the exhilarating insight which these recent generations have given to us, that *development* [i.e., modern progress] is *God's way of working out His will.* . . . When they say that Christ is coming, they mean that, slowly it may be, but surely, *His will and principles will be worked out . . . in human institutions*.[3]

Here we have what is at stake—the denial of the work of Christ and the actual return of Christ; the "new revelation" of modern thought replacing the Bible; salvation as the modern progress of human institutions. This is heretical denial of the gospel, and is directly related to the Enlightenment view of the perfectibility of Man.

Defending the Faith

In response to the wave of liberalism sweeping the denominations in the first three decades of this century, Bible-believing Christians tried to mount a spiritual defense of Christian truth. Here again the common understanding today is terribly distorted. The defense was led by some of the greatest minds and scholars of the day—men such as Benjamin B. Warfield, James Orr, W. H. Griffith Thomas, and G. Campbell Morgan. A key strategy in the defense was the publication of twelve paperback volumes from 1910 through 1915 called *The Fundamentals* and the later reissue of these in an edited four-volume set at the end of the decade. As one Christian historian pointed out recently, this was published as "a great 'Testimony to the Truth' and [was] even something of a scholarly *tour de force* . . . [which] assembled a rather formidable array of conservative American and British scholars . . . ."[4] Likewise, there was Dr. J. Gresham Machen, the distinguished professor of New Testament at Princeton Theological Seminary. In 1923 Machen published *Christianity and Liberalism*. In this brilliant defense of Christian truth Machen argued that liberalism was really a new religion and not Christianity at all. Since liberalism did not believe in the fact that Christ died in history to atone for the sins of men and women, and that this was the only basis for salvation, liberalism was really religious faith in man dressed up in Christian language and symbols. Thus, Machen explained, the only honest thing for the liberal to do would be to leave the churches which were founded on biblical truth.[5]

At the heart of the defense was the affirmation of the "essential fundamentals of the faith" by a broad base of Christian laymen and the defense of these by leading Christian scholars. The fundamentals themselves are usually identified in terms of five essential truths: 1) the inspiration and inerrancy of the Bible; 2) the deity of Christ and his virgin birth; 3) the substitutionary atonement of Christ's death; 4) the literal resurrection of Christ from the dead; and 5) the literal return of Christ.

Two Groups

As Bible-believing Christians today we have nothing to be ashamed of concerning the early "fundamentalists'" attempts to defend the truth of the gospel. Indeed, the specific doctrines which were defended as *The Fundamentals* are what have always been affirmed through the ages. And those defending them were Christian scholars of the highest order. But then in the 1930s something began to change. Prior to the 1930s the Bible-believing Christians had stood together as liberalism came in to steal the churches. Then at different speeds the liberals achieved their theft of the various denominations by gaining control of the power centers of the seminaries and the bureaucracies. At this point onward, Bible-believing Christians, instead of standing together, divided into two groups: those who held to the principle of the purity of the visible church, and those who accepted and acted upon the concept of a pluralistic church. There was a line just like that. It is a line that began back there in the 1930s, that has continued, and that marks the religious life of the United States excruciatingly to this day. On one hand there are those who hold to the principle of the purity of the visible church, and on the other hand those who accept the concept of the pluralistic church. Looking back over the years, we can see that there have been problems on both sides.

Looking first at those who affirmed the purity of the visible church and left the liberal denominations, we must admit there was often a hardness, a lack of love. It didn't have to be that way, but it was a mistake that marked the "separatist movement" for years to come. What happened in the Presbyterian Church in the United States (the Northern branch of the Presbyterian Church) was typical of what happened in most of the denominations. There were many who said before the division that they would not allow a liberal takeover. But when the time came, many of these remained in the denomination. It is true to say of those who came out, without judging their motives, that they felt deserted and betrayed. Some of those who stayed in the Northern Presbyterian Church urged that the Constitutional Convention Union—the vehicle for all of their working together previously—should not be dissolved, so as to enable those who stayed in and those who came out to continue to work together. But in exasperation and perhaps some anger, those who left dissolved it at once. All the lines of a practical example of observable love among the brethren were destroyed.

The periodicals of those who left tended to devote more space to attacking people who differed with them on the issue of leaving than to dealing with the liberals. Things were said that are difficult to forget even now. Those who came out refused at times to pray with those who had not come out. Many who left broke off all forms of fellowship with true brothers in Christ who had not left. Christ's command to love one another was destroyed. What was left was frequently a turning inward, a self-righteousness, a hardness. The impression often was left that coming out had made those who departed so right that anything could then be excused. Having learned such bad habits, they later treated each other badly when the resulting new groups had minor differences among themselves.

The Christian's Calling
In the midst of anger, frustration, and even self-righteousness, those who came out forgot what our calling as Christians always

must be. Our calling is to exhibit the existence of God and to exhibit his character, individually and collectively. God is holy and God is love, and our calling is simultaneously to show forth holiness and love in every aspect of life—as parent and child, as husband and wife, in business, in our Christian organizations, in the church, in government, in everything—an exhibition of the character of God showing forth his holiness and his love simultaneously. If we depend on the flesh rather than the work of the Spirit, it is easy to say we are showing holiness and yet it is only egotistic pride and hardness. Equally, in the flesh rather than the work of the Spirit, it is easy to say we are showing forth love and it is only egotistic compromise, latitudinarianism, and accommodation. Both are equally easy in the flesh. Both are equally egotistic. To show forth both simultaneously, in personal matters or in church and public life, can only be done in any real degree by our consciously bowing, denying our egotistic selves, and letting Christ bring forth his fruit through us—not merely as a "religious" statement, but with some ongoing reality.

Thus whenever it becomes necessary to draw a line in the defense of a central Christian truth it is so easy to be proud, to be hard. It is easy to be self-righteous and to self-righteously think that we are so right on this one point that anything else may be excused—this is very easy, a very easy thing to fall into. These mistakes were indeed made, and we have suffered from this and the cause of Christ has suffered from this through some fifty years. By God's grace, let us consciously look to our Lord for his help not to give Satan the victory by making this tragic error again.

The Real Chasm

A second problem of those who left the Presbyterian Church was a confusion over where to place the chasm that marks off our identity. Is the chasm placed between Bible-believing churches and those that are not? Or is it between those who are part of our own denomination and those who are not? When we go into a town to start a church, do we go there primarily motivated to build a church that is loyal to Presbyterianism and the Reformed faith, or to the Baptistic position on baptism, or to the Lutheran view of the sacraments, etc., etc.? Or do we go to build a church that will preach the gospel that historic, Bible-believing churches of all denominations hold, and then, on this side of that chasm, teach what we believe is true to the Bible with respect to our own denominational distinctives? The answers to these questions make a great deal of difference. There is a difference of motivation, of breadth and outreach. One view is catholic and biblical and gives promise of success—on two levels: first, in church growth and then a healthy outlook among those we reach; second, in providing leadership to the whole church of Christ. The other view is inverted and self-limiting—and sectarian.

As Bible-believing Christians we come from a variety of backgrounds. But in our moment of history we need each other. Let us keep our doctrinal distinctives. Let us talk to each other about them. But let us recognize the proper hierarchy of things. The real chasm is not between Presbyterians and everyone else, or Lutherans and everyone else, or Anglicans and everyone else, or Baptists and everyone else. The real chasm is between those who have bowed to the living God and thus also to the verbal, propositional communication of God's inerrant Word, the Scriptures, and those who have not.

Latitudinarianism

Now for those who did not leave the liberally controlled denominations fifty years ago, there were also two problems. First there was the birth of a general latitudinarianism—a kind of acceptance of theological pluralism which easily slips into compromise and accommodation. If those who came out were inclined to become hard, some of those who stayed in tended to become soft.

Some said: This is not the moment to come out, but we will do so if such-and-such occurs. These in principle did not accept the concept of a pluralistic church. Some developed their own kind of hardness—a decision to stay in, no matter what happened.

If one accepts an ecclesiastical latitudinarianism, it is easy to step into a cooperative latitudinarianism that easily encompasses doctrine, including one's view of Scripture. This is what happened historically. Out of the ecclesiastical latitudinarianism of the thirties and the forties has come the letdown with regard to Scripture in certain areas of evangelicalism in the eighties. Large sections of evangelicalism act as though it makes no real difference whether one holds the historic view of Scripture, or whether one holds the existential methodology that says the Bible is authoritative when it teaches religious things but not when it touches on what is historic or scientific, or on such things as the male/female relationship.

Not all who stayed in the liberal-dominated denominations have done this, by any means. I do not believe, however, that those who made the choice to stay in "no matter what happens" can escape a latitudinarian mentality. They will struggle to paper over the difference regarding Scripture so as to keep an external veneer of evangelical unity—when indeed today there is no unity at that crucial point of Scripture. When doctrinal latitudinarianism sets in, we can be sure both from church history and from personal observation that in one or two generations those who are taught by the churches and schools that hold this mentality will lose still more, and the line between evangelical and liberal will be lost.

Moving Back the Line

The second problem for those who did not leave the liberally controlled denominations is the natural tendency to continually move back the line at which the final stand must be taken. For example, could such well-known evangelical Presbyterians in the 1930s as Clarence McCartney, Donald Grey Barnhouse, and T. Roland Phillips have stayed in a denomination where there is no possibility of disciplining those who hold patently heretical views? Take for instance the case of Professor John Hick, the author of *The Myth of God Incarnate*. How can a man who holds that the Incarnation is a myth call himself a Christian? Yet he was recently received into the Presbytery of Claremont, California as a minister in good standing. How could these men have stayed in a denomination which takes a militantly proabortion stand? Or where it is considered a "victory" to have stalled the ordination of practicing homosexuals and lesbians? What do you think McCartney, Barnhouse, and Phillips would have said? Such a situation in their denomination would have been inconceivable to them.

False Victories

Evangelicals must be aware of false victories. The liberal denominational power structure knows how to keep Bible-believing Christians off balance. There are many possible false victories they can throw to evangelicals to prevent them from making a clear stand. There are still those who say, "Don't break up our ranks. Wait a while longer. Wait for this, wait for that." Always wait, never act. But fifty years is a long time to wait while things are getting worse. Because of my failing health, I am in a good position to say that we do not have forever to take that courageous and costly stand for Christ we sometimes talk about.

Even what seems to be a major victory may end up having no practical effect. Again, a clear example of this happened in the Northern Presbyterian Church. In 1924 the conservatives decided the best way to meet the liberal challenge was to elect a moderator of the General Assembly who would clearly be Bible-believing. As a result, 1924 saw elected as the moderator of the

Northern Presbyterian Church an orthodox, Bible-believing man, Dr. Clarence Edward McCartney. The conservatives were jubilant. The secular newspapers carried the story of the conservative victory, and the conservatives rejoiced. But while all the rejoicing was going on, the liberals consolidated their power in the church bureaucracy. And because they were allowed to do so, the election of the conservative moderator proved to mean nothing. By 1936 the liberals were so in control that they were able to defrock Dr. J. Gresham Machen, putting him out of the ministry.

It seems to me that by the end of the 1930s almost all the major Protestant denominations in the United States came under the control of those holding liberal theological views, and that now in the 1980s those denominations not dominated by liberal theology in the 1930s are in the same place of decision as the others were in the 1930s. It should be noted that the Roman Catholic Church now also has many in the hierarchy, many theologians and teachers, called progressives, who are existential theologians who believe and teach the same things as the existential theologians in the Protestant churches do, but using traditional Roman Catholic, rather than Protestant, terms.

Two of the Protestant denominations in the United States now in the place of decision, interestingly enough, have recently tried to protect themselves, as did the Northern Presbyterian Church, by electing a conservative executive officer. But I would urge the true Christian today in these denominations to learn from the mistakes of the Presbyterian Church. Do not think that merely because a Bible-believing man is elected as an executive officer or is appointed to an important position, this will give safety to a denomination. If the two power centers in modern denominations—the bureaucracy and the seminaries—remain in the control of the liberals, nothing will be permanently changed. There must be a loving but definite *practice* of the purity of the visible church in any denomination if it is really to dwell in safety. The holiness of God must be exhibited in ecclesiastical affairs. We must practice truth, not just speak about it.

Flaming Truth

It must be understood that the new humanism and the new theology have no concept of true truth—absolute truth. Relativism has triumphed in the church as well as in the university and in society. The true Christian, however, is called upon not only to teach truth, but to practice truth in the midst of such relativism. And if we are ever to practice truth, it certainly must be in a day such as ours.

This means, among other things, that after we have done all we can on a personal level, if the liberals in the church persist in their liberalism, they should come under discipline. As I have shown at length in *The Church Before the Watching World*, the church must remain the faithful bride of Christ.[6] And, as I explained there in detail, the liberals are not faithful to the God of the Bible, the God who is there.[7] Historic Christianity, biblical Christianity, believes that Christianity is not just doctrinal truth, but flaming truth—true to what is there, true to the great final environment, the infinite-personal God. Liberalism, on the other hand, is unfaithfulness; *it is spiritual adultery toward the divine Bridegroom.* We are involved, therefore, in a matter of loyalty— loyalty not only to the creeds, but to the Scripture, and beyond that to the divine Bridegroom—the infinite-personal divine Bridegroom who is there in an absolute antithesis to his not being there.

We not only believe in the existence of truth, but we believe we have the truth—a truth that has content and can be verbalized (and *then* can be lived)—a truth we can share with the twentieth-century world. Christ and the Bible have given us this truth. Do you think our contemporaries will take us seriously if we do not practice truth? Do you think for a moment that the really serious-minded twentieth-century young people—our own youth as they go off to universities, who are taught in the fields of sociology, psychology, philosophy, etc., that all is relative—will they take us seriously if we do not *practice* truth in very practical ways? In an age that does not believe that truth exists, do you really believe they will take seriously that their parents are speaking truth and believe in truth? Will their parents have credibility if they do not practice antithesis in religious matters?

It is therefore necessary for the true Christians in the church to oppose McLuhanesque "cool" communication employed by the liberal theologians with the "hot" communication of theological and biblical content. It is only thus that we can practice the exhibition of the holiness of God.

We believe in the hot communication of content, and as our age cools off more and more in its communication, as content is played down and reason is plowed under, I believe the historic Christian faith must more and more consciously emphasize content, content, and then more content. In this we are brought face-to-face in a complete antithesis with the existential theologian. If we are to talk truth at all, we must have content on the basis of antithesis; and to do this, we must have discipline with regard to those who depart from the historic Christian faith. It is thus that we can practice the exhibition of the holiness of God.

At the same time, however, we must show forth the love of God to those with whom we differ. Fifty years ago in the Presbyterian crisis in the United States, we forgot that. We did not speak with love about those with whom we differed, and we have been paying a price for it ever since. We must love men, including the existential theologians, even if they have given up content entirely. We must deal with them as our neighbors, for Christ gave us the second commandment telling us that we are to love all men as our neighbors.

We must stand clearly for the principle of the purity of the visible church, and we must call for the appropriate discipline of those who take a position which is not according to Scripture. But at the same time we must visibly love them as people as we speak and write about them. We must show it before both the church and the world. We must say that the liberals are desperately wrong and that they require discipline in and by the church, but we must do so in terms that show it is not merely the flesh speaking. This is beyond us, but not beyond the work of the Holy Spirit. I regret that years ago we did not do this in the Presbyterian Church; we did not talk of the need to show love as we stood against liberalism. And as the Presbyterian Church was lost, that lack has cost us dearly.

The Tragedy of Bishop Pike

But with prayer, both love and concern for truth can be shown. Several years ago at the Roosevelt University auditorium in Chicago, I had a dialogue with Bishop James Pike. (Bishop Pike was a leading liberal in the Episcopal Church.) Some years before our dialogue, he had been brought to trial in the Episcopal Church on heresy charges. However, the charges were eventually dropped—not because his views were in fact orthodox, but because the Episcopal denomination had accepted theological pluralism and relativism and therefore had no real basis upon which to practice discipline.

Before the dialogue, I asked those in L'Abri to pray for one thing—that I would be able to present a clear Christian position to him and to the audience, and at the same time end with a good human relationship between the two of us. It was something I could not do in myself, but God answered that prayer. A clear statement was raised, with a clear statement of differences, without destroying him as a human being. At the close he said,

"If you ever come to California, please visit me in Santa Barbara." Later, when Edith and I were out in Santa Barbara, we went to his place and were able to carry on further a discussion with him without one iota of compromise, and yet again not destroying him, but letting him know that we respected him as a human being.

We also talked about the possibility that his belief that he was talking to his son "on the other side" was really a matter of demonology. This was some time after Bishop Pike's son had committed suicide, and he had tried to communicate with his son through a medium. And he did not get angry, though he was close to crying. It is possible to make clear statements, even the necessary negative ones, if simultaneously we treat people as people.

I will never forget the last time I saw him as Edith and I were leaving the Center for the Study of Democratic Institutions. He said one of the saddest things I have ever heard: "When I turned from being agnostic, I went to Union Theological Seminary, eager for and expecting bread; but when I graduated, all that it left me was a handful of pebbles."

Who is responsible for the tragedy of Bishop James Pike? His liberal theological professors who robbed him of everything real and human. We cannot take lightly the fact that liberal theological professors in any theological school are leaving young men and women with a handful of pebbles and nothing more.

Yet, even in the midst of this situation, by God's grace we must do two things simultaneously. We must do all that is necessary for the purity of the visible church to exhibit the holiness of God; and yet, no matter how bitter the liberals become or what nasty things they say or what they release to the press, we must show forth the love of God in the midst of the strongest speaking we can do. If we let down one side or the other, we will not bear our testimony to God who is holy and who is love.

Discipline

Let us again go back to the Presbyterian struggles of the thirties when true Christians did not remember to keep this balance. On the one hand, they waited far too long to exert discipline, and so they lost the denomination, as did the Christians in almost every other denomination. On the other hand, some of them treated the liberals as less than human, and therefore they learned such bad habits that later, when those who formed new groups developed minor differences among themselves, they continued to treat each other badly. Beware of the habits we learn in controversy. Both must appear together: the holiness of God and the love of God exhibited simultaneously by the grace of God. It will not come automatically. It takes prayer. We must write about it in our denominational papers. We must talk about it to our congregations; we must preach sermons pointing out the necessity of standing for the holiness of God and the love of God *simultaneously*, and by our attitudes we must *exhibit* it to our congregations and to our own children.

It is important to notice the principle we are speaking about here and the language we use to express that principle. It is not the principle of *separation*. It is the *practice of the principle of the purity of the visible church*. Words are important at this point, because we make attitudes with the words we choose and use year after year. So I repeat: the principle is the practice of the purity of the visible church. That principle may have to be exhibited in various ways, but that is the principle. The church belongs to those who by the grace of God are faithful to the Scriptures. Almost every church has in its history a process for exercising discipline, and when needed this should be used in the practice of the positive principle.

Between the 1890s and the 1930s we can see how the practice of discipline was turned on its head. In the early 1890s, disciplinary action was taken against Dr. Charles A. Briggs. Dr.

Briggs was a vigorous advocate of higher criticism and a leader in the introduction of liberalism to Union Theological Seminary in New York. In 1881 he was tried for heresy and was eventually suspended from the ministry in 1883 by the General Assembly of the Northern Presbyterian Church. But by the 1930s the older type of liberals had taken over the denomination, and the situation was completely reversed. In 1936 the *liberals* were able to put Dr. Machen out of the denomination for his firm and practical stand for orthodoxy in belief and practice.

Dr. Machen was disciplined and put out of the ministry. What had happened in the intervening years? Discipline had not been consistently applied by the faithful men of the church. The church was able to discipline Dr. Briggs in the 1880s, but after that faithful men waited too long. Though they had achieved one outstanding victory, after that first burst of discipline they did nothing, until it was far too late. Discipline in the church and in our Christian organizations—as in the family—is not something that can be done in one great burst of enthusiasm, one great conference, one great anything. Men must be treated in love as human beings, but it is a case of continual, moment-by-moment care, for we are not dealing with a merely human organization but with the church of Christ. Hence, the practice of the purity of the visible church first means discipline of those who do not take a proper position in regard to the teaching of Scripture.

Why is it so unthinkable today to have discipline? Why is it that at least two denominations in the United States are now so much in the hands of liberals that it is officially and formally no longer possible to have a discipline trial, ever—even in theory? It is because both the world and the liberal church are totally caught up in the grasp of synthesis and relativism. It was not unthinkable to our forefathers to conduct discipline hearings, because they believed that truth existed. But because the world and the liberal church no longer believe in truth as truth, any concept of discipline in regard to doctrine has become unthinkable.

A Second Step

Let us now shift our focus. What does the future hold? What can we expect for ourselves, our congregations, our physical and spiritual children in the days ahead? America is moving at great speed toward a totally humanistic society and state. Do we suppose this trend will leave our own little projects, lives, and churches untouched? When a San Francisco Orthodox Presbyterian congregation can be dragged into court for breaking the law against discrimination because it dismissed an avowed, practicing homosexual as an organist, can we be so deaf as not to hear all the warning bells?

In what presbytery in the Presbyterian Church U.S.A. can you bring an ordained man under biblical discipline for holding false views of doctrine and expect him to be disciplined? The same is true in many other denominations. We should first of all, of course, do all we can on a personal, loving level to help the liberal; but if he persists in his liberalism he should be brought under discipline, because the visible church should remain the faithful bride of Christ.

The church is not the world. When a denomination comes to a place where such discipline cannot operate, then before the Lord her members must consider a second step: that step, with regard to the practice of the principle of the purity of the visible church, is with tears to step out. Not with flags flying, not with shouts of hurrah or thoughts that in this fallen world we can build a perfect church, but that step is taken with tears.

Evangelicals who come to this point must still keep on loving the liberals, and must do so because it is right. If we do not know how to take a firm stand against organized liberalism and still love the liberals, we have failed in half of the call to exhibit simultaneously the love and the holiness of God—

before a watching world, before a watching church, before our children, before the watching angels, and before the face of the Lord himself.

Learning from the Past

As we face the watershed issue concerning the full authority and inerrancy of the Scriptures, what can we learn from the past? First, we must recognize that there is a direct parallel between what happened in the early decades of this century and what we are facing today. Will we repeat the mistakes we made in the past, or will we learn from these and remain faithful to God by simultaneously expressing his love and holiness?

Within the evangelical circles things are moving rapidly in the direction of what happened fifty years ago in the denominations. But there still is time to head off a complete takeover of the leadership and key organizations within evangelicalism by those who hold a weakened view of Scripture and have been infiltrated theologically and culturally by the surrounding world view—if we have the courage to clearly but lovingly draw a line. Sadly though, we must say that things *are* moving rapidly and in precisely the same way that the denominations went some fifty years ago. There is the growing acceptance of higher critical methods in our colleges and seminaries. There is a growing acceptance of the neo-orthodox existential methodology. There is a growing infiltration of humanistic ideas into both *theology and practice*. There is a growing acceptance of pluralism and accommodation. And what has been the response of the evangelical leadership? Overwhelmingly it has been to keep silent, to let the slide go further and further, to paper over the differences. Here again we see the great evangelical disaster—the failure of the evangelical leadership to take a stand really on anything that would stand decisively over against the relativistic moral slide of our culture—the failure to take a stand on anything that would "rock the boat" concerning our personal projects and acceptance. And now when our culture is all but lost, can we expect anything but further disaster in the form of a complete moral breakdown and the rise of a new humanistic authoritarianism if we do not take a stand?

Practical Steps

On a very practical level, in our evangelical organizations and institutions, as well as our churches and denominations, we will need to take some very specific steps. Where there is a departure from the historic view of Scripture and from obedience to God's Word, then those who take this weakened view need to be brought under discipline. It must be done according to all that has been said so far in this chapter—with genuine love, without self-righteousness, and everything else that I have said. But a clear line must be drawn—by those who sit on the boards of evangelical organizations and colleges and seminaries; when we recommend schools for students to attend or avoid; when we are asked to work together for the sake of the gospel with others who hold a weakened view of the Bible; when we decide who and what we will publish in our magazines and publishing houses. In organizations such as these, and especially in the colleges and seminaries, the issues are crucial. For it was the failure of evangelicals fifty years ago to practice discipline and maintain control of the denominational centers of influence—in colleges and seminaries, in publishing, and in the organizational structures—which allowed the liberals to take control.

And if the moment should come for you when loyalty to Christ brings you to the place of bringing discipline to bear, or even to leaving your local church or denomination or Christian organization, I plead with you to find some way to show observable love among *true* Christians before the world. The practice of truth requires that a line be drawn between those who hold the historic view of Scripture and the new weaker one. But this is not to say that those who hold this view are not often brothers and sisters in Christ, nor that we should not have loving personal relationships with them. Don't just divide into ugly parties. If you do, the world will see an ugliness which will turn it off. Your children will see the ugliness, and you will lose some of your sons and daughters. They will hear such harsh things from your lips against men who they know have been your friends that they will turn away from you. Don't throw your children away; don't throw other people away by forgetting to observe, by God's grace, the two principles simultaneously—to show love and holiness.

When the World Is on Fire

Finally, we must not forget that the world is on fire. We are not only losing the church, but our entire culture as well. We live in the post-Christian world which is under the judgment of God. I believe today that we must speak as Jeremiah did. Some people think that just because the United States of America is the United States of America, because Britain is Britain, they will not come under the judgment of God. This is not so. I believe that we of Northern Europe since the Reformation have had such light as few others have ever possessed. We have stamped upon that light in our culture. Our cinemas, our novels, our art museums, our schools scream out as they stamp upon that light. And worst of all, modern theology screams out as it stamps upon that light. Do you think God will not judge our countries simply because they are our countries? Do you think that the holy God will not judge?

And if this is true in our moment of history, we need each other. Let us keep our denominational distinctives. And let us talk to each other about our distinctives as we keep them.

But in a day like ours, let us recognize a proper hierarchy of things. Our distinctives are not to be the chasm. We hold our distinctives because we are convinced that they are biblical. But

God's call is to love and be one with all those who are in Christ Jesus, and then to let God's truth speak into the whole spectrum of life and the whole spectrum of society. That is our calling. The limiting circle is not to be the distinctives of our own particular denomination. We hold these things because we believe indeed they are taught in Scripture. But beyond that there is the responsibility, there is the call, to be something to the whole church of the Lord Jesus Christ, and beyond the church of the Lord Jesus Christ to the whole society and to the whole culture. If we don't understand this, we understand neither how rich Christianity is and God's truth is, nor do we understand how wide is the call placed upon the Christian into the totality of life. Jesus cannot be said to be Savior unless we also say he is Lord. And we cannot honestly and rightly say he is our Lord if he is only a Lord of part of life and not of the totality of life, including all the social and political and cultural life.

In a day like ours, when the world is on fire, let us be careful to keep things in proper order. We must have the courage to draw the line between those who have compromised the full authority of the Scriptures, either by *theological infiltration* or *cultural infiltration*, and those who have not. But we must at the same time practice an observable oneness among all who have bowed to the living God and thus to the verbal propositional communication of God's Word, the Scriptures. Learning from the mistakes of the past, let us raise a testimony that may still turn both the churches and society around—for the salvation of souls, the building of God's people, and at least the slowing down of the slide toward a totally humanistic society and an authoritarian suppressive state.

PART III:

NAMES AND ISSUES

CHAPTER 4

Connotations and Compromise

Names are funny things, and especially in the connotations
they are given. Names can be used either to enhance or
to destroy.

As we have seen in the preceding chapter, the name "fundamentalism" first came into use in the mid-1920s. During this
time and before, liberalism was sweeping through the major denominations and the liberals were taking over the positions of
leadership and control in the seminaries, in many Christian publications, and in the denominational structures.

Fundamental Truths

In response, the Bible-believing Christians, under the leadership
of such scholars as J. Gresham Machen and Robert Dick Wil-
son, issued what they called *The Fundamentals of the Faith*. Dr.
Machen and the other men never thought of making this an "ism."
They considered these things to be a true expression of the his-

toric Christian faith and doctrine. They were the *fundamental truths of the Christian faith*—doctrine which was true to the Bible; *truth* which they were interested in and committed to. And as we have seen in the preceding chapter, this truth was presented and published in a series of books written by the outstanding Christian thinkers of the day. Dr. Machen, whom I knew as a student, simply called himself a "Bible-believing Christian." The same thing was true of the many publications which were also committed in that day to doctrine and teaching which is true to the Bible.

Soon however, the word *fundamentalist* came into use. As used at first, it had nothing problematic in its use either in definition or in connotation. I personally, however, preferred Machen's term "Bible-believing Christian" because that was what the discussion was all about.

As time passed, however, the term *fundamentalist* took on a connotation for many people which had no necessary relationship to its original meaning. It came to connote a form of pietism which shut Christian interest up to only a very limited view of spirituality. In this new connotation, many things having to do with the arts, culture, education, and social involvement were considered to be "unspiritual" and not a proper area of concern for the Christian. Spirituality had to do with a very narrow sphere of the Christian's life, and all other things were considered to be suspect. Fundamentalism also, at times, became overly harsh and lacking in love, while properly saying that the liberal doctrine that was false to the Bible had to be met with confrontation.

The Full Spectrum of Life
Therefore, at a certain point in this country a new name was entered—*evangelical*. This was picked up largely from the British scene. In Britain during the twenties and thirties, *evangelical* largely meant what Machen and the others had stood for in this country—namely, Bible-believing Christianity as opposed to the

inroads of various forms and degrees of liberal theology. By the mid-1940s the name *evangelical* had come into common use in the United States. It was especially used here with the connotation of being Bible-believing without shutting one's self off from the full spectrum of life, and in trying to bring Christianity into effective contact with the current needs of society, government, and culture. It had a connotation of leading people to Christ as Savior, but then trying to be salt and light in the culture.

It was in this general period that my lectures and books began to be of some influence—from the 1950s onward. My lectures and early books stressed the Lordship of Christ over all of life in the areas of culture, art, philosophy, and so on while also strongly stressing the need to be Bible-believing with loving but true confrontation against not only false theology, but also against the destructive results of the false world view about us.

While not overemphasizing their importance, for many of that period and especially in the radical sixties, these books did help open a new door. Many discovered a Christianity which is viable in this age of collapsing values when the older cultural norms are being turned on their heads by the ethos dominating our age. And many came to understand that this new ethos— namely, the concept that the final reality is energy which has existed forever in some form and takes its present form by chance— has totally destructive consequences for life. The young people of the sixties sensed that this position left all standards in a relativistic flux and life as meaningless, and they began to think and live in these terms. In this setting, happily a certain number did find that L'Abri's presentation of Christianity—as touching all of thought and life, along with a life of prayer—did demonstrate Christianity's viability, and they became Bible-believing, consecrated Christians.

But note: this rested upon two things: 1) being truly Bible-believing; and 2) facing the results of the surrounding wrong world view that was current with loving but definite confrontation. By the grace of God this emphasis had some influence in many countries and in many disciplines.

Now, however, we find this matter of names with their connotations entering again. Gradually, though there was no need for it from the original use of the word, an appreciable section of those known as evangelical began a drift toward *accommodation*. Note, there was no need for this from the original use of the word, nor largely from the stance of the men and women who originally had begun to use the word. Those who originally called themselves evangelicals were both Bible-believing and did not take a compromising position in relation to the world.

The "Blue Jean" Mentality

It is important to see what the effect of this has been. This drift toward accommodation is a kind of mirror situation of what occurred previously with fundamentalism. After the denominational turmoil of the thirties, fundamentalism fell increasingly into a mistaken pietism which saw any challenge to the surrounding culture as unspiritual—that the Christian's job was only to lead people to Christ and then to know something of a personalized Christianity. Thus, the changing, destructive surrounding culture tended to stand increasingly unchallenged. In the case of an accommodating evangelicalism, there has been a tendency to talk about a wider, richer Christianity and to become more deeply involved in culture, but at the same time to accommodate to the world spirit about us at each crucial point. Note that the result is then the same. Despite claims of cultural relevance, an accommodating evangelicalism also leaves the destructive surrounding culture increasingly unchallenged. Thus the two positions end up with similar results.

This rather reminds me of young people whom we worked with at Berkeley and other universities, including certain Christian colleges, and those who came to us in large numbers with packs on their backs at L'Abri in the 1960s. They were rebels. They knew they were, for they wore the rebel's mark—the worn-out blue jeans. But they did not seem to notice that the blue jeans had become the mark of accommodation—that indeed, everyone was in blue jeans. This does seem to me to be a close parallel to what we see in much of the connotation which grew out of the new uses of the word *evangelical*. What they are saying is this: "We are the 'new evangelicals,' the 'open evangelicals'; we have thrown off the cultural isolation and anti-intellectualism of the old fundamentalists." But what they have not noticed is that they have nothing to say which stands in clear confrontation and antithesis to the surrounding culture. It is so easy to be a radical in the wearing of blue jeans when it fits in with the general climate of wearing blue jeans.

This is really nothing new. Christianity has been plagued by accommodation time and again through the centuries, and in particular in this century. It is interesting to note what Dr. Harold J. Ockenga wrote about the liberalism at the turn of this century:

> Destructive higher criticism of the Bible became the dominant approach among the theologians at the close of the nineteenth century and during the early twentieth century. When joined with naturalistic evolution, it produced liberalism. . . . It [liberalism] *accommodated Christianity to modern scientific naturalism* . . . whenever objections arose on the details of the Christian religion.[1]

It is interesting to note further that even some liberals have begun to recognize the devastating effect of theological accommodation and are beginning to grow weary of it and are wondering what to do. One such liberal recently wrote:

> The central theme of contemporary theology is *accommodation to modernity*. It is the underlying motif that unites the seemingly vast differences between existential theology, process theology, liberation theology, demythologization, and many varieties of liberal theology—all are searching for some more compatible adjustment to modernity.
>
> *The spirit of accommodation has...[led to] the steady deterioration of a hundred years and the disaster of the last two decades...*[2]

Yet accommodation has become fashionable among many evangelicals—in spite of the devastating effect this has had theologically and culturally.

Holiness and Love

Complicating the matter is our own tendency to lack a proper balance. As we confront the issues, there must be a proper balance under the leadership of the Holy Spirit while carefully living within the circle of that which is taught in Scripture. Each issue must be met with holiness and love simultaneously. To be really Bible-believing and true to our living Christ, each issue demands a balance which says "no" to two opposite errors: we can neither compromise love in the name of holiness; nor can we compromise holiness in the name of love. Or to say it another way: the devil never gives us the luxury of fighting the battle on just one front.

In every generation God calls his people to show forth his love and holiness, to be faithful to him, and to stand against accommodation with the world's values of the day. In order to show forth God's love and holiness and to present the Good News to

68252

our generation in such a way that the message has viability, we must try in a balanced way not to fall into the "blue-jean" mistake of thinking that we are courageous and "being with it" when we are really only fitting into what is the accepted thought-form of the age around us.

We must admit we have not done well here. And I do not think that the evangelical leaders in positions of influence—in schools, in publishing, in other spheres of influence—have been helpful in these things. All too often, it seems to me that "being with it" simply has meant dealing with the current popular topics, but really not being in balanced but clear confrontation with them. This, of course, is in line with the spirit of relativism that dominates in our age. Since the prevailing world view teaches that the final reality is a silent universe which can give no value judgments, truth as final truth therefore does not exist. Thus, there can be various differences of personal opinions, but not the confrontation of truth versus error, as not only the Christians but also the classical philosophers and thinkers of the past believed to be the case. We are left with no basis for saying something is right or wrong. Thus when confronting the crucial issues of the day, the prevailing world view teaches that there is neither right nor wrong, only personal opinion. Relativism rules, and we are surrounded by a spirit of accommodation.

"Don't Rock the Boat"

The matter of human life is a good case in point. "I am personally against abortion, but...." with any number of qualifications added—this became the mediating phrase not only of Christians in government, but also of many in the pulpit and in publications as well. The end result is the same as moral relativism; the issue of abortion is reduced to a personal opinion which has no relationship to the way one lives one's life in the world. In the mid-1970s when Dr. C. Everett Koop, Franky Schaeffer, and I began to work on the project *Whatever Happened to the Human Race?* there were in fact so few Protestants involved that the battle was being lost simply by its being called a Roman Catholic issue. Why were there so few Protestants involved? The mistaken pietists thought battles in the area of government were "unspiritual"; the other stream had acquired the habit of accommodation and it would have meant "rocking the boat" badly to take a clear stand. Happily more are committed now, but still the damage has been done. If voices had been clearly raised in confrontation when abortion and the general lowering of the view of human life began to be openly advocated, the original flood of these concepts in all probability could not have prevailed and the *Roe* v. *Wade* ruling by the Supreme Court might never have been made. And if the heat had been kept on by Christian leaders and publications, the Christians who are in Congress would not have found it so convenient to say they were personally against abortion, but then, for example, vote against limitations on government funding of abortions.

It is ironic that so many who were opposed to Christianity's being shut up to a removed and isolated spirituality by a poor pietism now have by a process of accommodation ended up just as silently on all those issues which go against the current commonly accepted thought-forms. It is so easy to be radical in wearing blue jeans when it fits into a general wearing of blue jeans.

Truth really does bring forth confrontation—loving confrontation, but confrontation—whether it is in regard to those who take a lower view of the Scriptures than both the original users of the terms "fundamentalist" and "evangelical" took, or in regard to holding a lower view of human life. This lowering of the view of human life may begin with talking about extreme cases in regard to abortion, but it flows on to infanticide and on to all of human life being open to arbitrary, pragmatic judgments of what human life is worthy to be lived—including your human life when you become a burden to society.

In the preceding chapter I quoted from a letter from a Christian leader which tied the issue of Scripture and abortion. I would stress again what I said there—that on the basis of what the word *evangelical* originally meant in regard to Scripture, we must be willing in love to draw a line in regard to those who take a lowered view of Scripture. On the basis of the original term *evangelical,* they are false evangelicals. Not to do so is accommodation to the world's spirit about us at a crucial point which will eventually carry everything else down with it.

But the same principle applies equally in the crucial issues of human life. A lowered view of life and a lowered view of Scripture go hand-in-hand. The watershed issue is *obedience to the Bible* just as much as it is belief in the doctrine of inerrancy. Since the Bible teaches that life in the womb is human life, one cannot accept abortion without denying the authority and truth of Scripture in practice. In drawing or not drawing a line on the issue of Scripture, and indeed in regard to human life, the evangelical establishment has also produced little or no leadership. Most of the time they seem to understand nothing in regard to the real issue involved. Either from a false practice of pietism or a fear of rocking their own boat, they have not been evident in the fray at this crucial point of the question of human life. Or if at all, they have come very late into the battle.

The Real Issue

It is curious how the world often seems to understand these issues better than most Christians and Christian leaders. For example, a recent essay in *Time* magazine entitled "Thinking Animal Thoughts" spells out the real issue. In discussing "animal rights," *Time* tries to discover whether or not there is really any difference between animal life and human life:

If human beings assume that they were created in the image of God, it is not difficult for them to see the vast and qualitative distance between themselves and the lesser orders of creation. The Bible teaches that man has dominion over the fish of the sea, the fowl of the air, the cattle and every creeping thing. Perhaps the rise of the animal rights movement is a symptom of a more secular and self-doubting spirit....

The human difference is known, to some, as the immortal soul, an absolute distinction belonging to man and woman alone, not to the animal. The soul is the human pedigree—and presumably the dispensation to slay and eat any inferior life that crosses the path. *But in a secular sense how is human life different from animal life?* Intelligence? Some pygmy chimps and even lesser creatures are as intelligent as, say, a severely retarded child; if it is not permissible to kill a retarded child, why kill the animals?[3]

Thus *Time* points out that when we take away the biblical teaching that God is the final reality and that God created man uniquely in his own image, then man as man has no intrinsic value. In a secular sense, human life is no different from animal life. Or in other words, when one accepts the secular world view that the final reality is only material or energy shaped by chance, then human life is lowered to the level of animal existence. There are only two classifications—nonlife and life. And if one thinks of human life as basically no different from animal life, why not treat people the same way? It would only be religious nostalgia to do otherwise. And so it first becomes easy to kill children in the womb, and then if one does not like the way they turn out, to kill children after they are born. And then it goes on to the euthanasia of anyone who becomes a burden or inconvenience.

After all, according to the secular world view, human life is not intrinsically different from animal life—so why should it be treated differently?

One would have wished the Christian press and Christian leaders would have had the same comprehension as *Time* and seen these implications. But on the few occasions when secularism and secular humanism have been dealt with, has the Christian press exposed the real implications of this world view? One Christian magazine came out with the conclusion that the concern over secular humanism and its resulting impact on society was only a bogeyman.[4] Rightly defined, secular humanism—or humanism, or secularism, or whatever name you may wish to use—is no bogeyman; it is a vicious enemy. Here again balance is important by means of careful definition. The word *humanism* is not to be confused with humanitarianism, nor with the word humanities.[5] But humanism is the defiant denial of the God who is there, with Man defiantly set up in the place of God as the measure of all things. For if the final reality is only material or energy which has existed forever and has its present form only by chance, then there is no one but finite man to set purely relative values and a purely relativistic base for law and government. This is no bogeyman! It stands totally against all that the original fundamentalists stood for, and totally against what the original meaning of evangelical stood for, and totally against all that the Bible stands for. How could any Christian be so foolish as not to see that this "bogeyman" *guarantees destruction to the individual in the life to come, and in the present life as well?*

Religious Mumbo Jumbo

Do you realize what the implications of this are? Do you really understand that the biblical view of man and the secularist view are a total antithesis—and as such, they result in a totally conflicting view of human life, with totally different consequences?

The secular world understands this, as can be seen clearly in the comments of Dr. Peter Singer. Writing in the prestigious medical journal *Pediatrics,* Dr. Singer explains:

> The ethical outlook that holds human life to be sac-rosanct—I shall call it the "sanctity-of-life view"—is under attack. The first major blow to the sanctity-of-life view was the spreading acceptance of abortion throughout the Western world. Supporters of the sanctity-of-life view have pointed out that some premature babies are less developed than some of the fetuses that are killed in late abortions. They add, very plausibly, that the location of the fetus/infant—inside or outside the womb—cannot make a crucial difference to its moral status. Allowing abortions, especially these late abortions, therefore does seem to breach our defense of the allegedly universal sanctity of innocent human life.
>
> A second blow to the sanctity-of-life view has been the revelation that it is standard practice in many major public hospitals to refrain from providing necessary life-saving treatment to certain patients. . . .
>
> Is the erosion of the sanctity-of-life view really so alarming? Change is often, in itself, alarming, especially change in something that for centuries has been spoken of in such hushed tones that to question it is automatically to commit sacrilege. . . .
>
> Whatever the future holds, it is likely to prove impossible to restore in full the sanctity-of-life view. The philosophical foundations of this view have been knocked asunder. We can no longer base our ethics on the idea that human beings are a special form of creation, made in the image of God, singled out from all

other animals, and alone possessing an immortal soul. Our better understanding of our own nature has bridged the gulf that was once thought to lie between ourselves and other species, so why should we believe that the mere fact that a being is a member of the species *Homo sapiens* endows its life with some unique, almost infinite, value?

Once the religious mumbo jumbo surrounding the term "human" has been stripped away, we may continue to see normal members of our species as possessing greater capacities of rationality, self-consciousness, communication, and so on, than members of any other species, but we will not regard as sacrosanct the life of each and every member of our species, no matter how limited its capacity for intelligent or even conscious life may be. If we compare a severely defective human infant with a nonhuman animal, a dog or a pig, for example, we will often find the nonhuman to have superior capacities, both actual and potential, for rationality, self-consciousness, communication, and anything else that can plausibly be considered morally significant. Only the fact that the defective infant is a member of the species *Homo sapiens* leads it to be treated differently from the dog or pig. Species membership alone, however, is not morally relevant. . . .

If we can put aside the obsolete and erroneous notion of the sanctity of all human life, we may start to look at human life as it really is: at the quality of life that each human being has or can achieve. Then it will be possible to approach these difficult questions of life and death with the ethical sensitivity that each case demands, rather than with the blindness to individual differences that is embodied in the Department of Health and Human Services' rigid instruction to disregard all handicaps when deciding whether to keep a child alive.[6]

Do you understand what you have just read? If you take away the biblical teaching of the sanctity of human life and of man created in the image of God (as Dr. Singer has shown so clearly), there is no final basis for placing value on human life. And this applies whether we are talking about the unborn or those who are already born. If human life can be taken before birth, there is no logical reason why it cannot be taken after birth. Thus the quality of life, arbitrarily judged by fallible and sinful people, becomes the standard for killing or not killing human life— whether unborn, newly born, the rich, or the aged. But what then does this say about the handicapped now alive? Isn't their life wrongly and tragically devalued? There are people who will read this book who would be allowed to die under these criteria if they were born today.[7]

The question of human life truly is a watershed issue. Those who accept abortion try to conceal the horrible reality behind respectable language such as the "quality of life," or "the happiness and well-being of the mother," or "the need for every child to be wanted." Although such language may sound close to what the Bible teaches—that all human life is created in the image of God and as such has unique, intrinsic value—it results in the total devaluation of life. The unborn child is a human being created in the image of God, and to deny this is to deny the authority of the Bible. It is impossible to read Psalm 139 and truly believe what it says without realizing that life in the womb is human life. It is impossible to truly believe in the Incarnation and not realize that the child conceived in Mary by the power of the Holy Spirit was indeed the Son of God from the time of conception. If we

truly believe the Bible, there is no question when human life begins.[8] And to deny this is to deny the authority of the Bible.

But the question is not just abortion, as important as that
is. Are we so blind not to see what is involved? It is human life
as human life that is involved. Yet much of the evangelical world
carries on business as usual, saying they are not for abortion except for this or that; or saying that we should not make an issue
of this because it might be divisive; or saying we should not draw
a line—even when millions of human lives are at stake. *But if
we are not willing to take a stand even for human life, is there
anything for which we will stand?*

CHAPTER 5

Forms of the World Spirit

It is comfortable to accommodate to that which is in vogue about us, to the forms of the world spirit in our age. This accommodation has been deadly—in the loss of twelve million human lives over the last ten years by abortion. But it does not stop with questions of human life; it is just as evident on virtually every other issue which has been made fashionable by the secularist mentality of the day.

The Socialistic Mentality

Thus in another area we find that a large section of evangelicalism is confusing the kingdom of God with a socialistic program. This too is sheer accommodation to the world spirit around us. A clear example can be found in a newsletter published by a leading evangelical magazine. In a recent issue the newsletter featured the work of Evangelicals for Social Action (ESA), their social strategy, and their critique of society. As ESA explains:

Summarized briefly, this critique claims that the social problems Christians in this nation are most concerned about (i.e., crime, abortion, lack of prayer, secular humanism, etc.) are important, but are actually symptoms of much larger problems—*unjust social structures in the United States*—which underlie these legitimate Christian concerns.

The obvious answer, then, is to attack the causes of the disease so the symptoms will go away. ESA spends much of its educational effort trying to acquaint biblical Christians with crucial areas of basic injustices in society and the need to change these for the better.

What are these basic "unjust structures"? ESA believes that most of them (but certainly not all) stem from poverty and the maldistribution of wealth, both on the national and international levels.[1]

Do you understand what is being said here? Remarkably, ESA is saying that "unjust social structures" and in particular "the maldistribution of wealth" are the real causes of evil in the world. According to ESA it is these things (e.g., unjust social structures/maldistribution of wealth) which cause "crime, abortion, lack of prayer, secular humanism, etc." Just on a factual level this is foolish. There is crime at all levels of society irrespective of wealth; abortion is supported most strongly by the wealthy. And does ESA really believe that changing economic structures would solve the problem of "lack of prayer"? Here the gospel has been reduced to a program for transforming social structures. This is the Marxist line. It does not mean that those who take this position are Communists. But it does mean they have made a complete confusion of the kingdom of God with the basic socialistic concepts. In back of this stands the Enlightenment idea of the perfectibility of man if only the cultural and economic chains are removed.[2]

But think further what this means theologically. What has happened to the fall and sin? ESA seems to be saying that changing economic structures is the means of salvation for modern man since only this deals with the basic "causes of the disease." Ironically their program is not radical enough! The basic problem is that of the fall and sin and the heart of man. The basic problem is much deeper than social structures, and by not recognizing this ESA ends up with an understanding of salvation which is very different from what the Scriptures teach. Sin is the problem, and there is no greater sin than modern man's willful defiance of God and his laws both in the area of ideas and actions.

The socialist mentality as promoted by Evangelicals for Social Action and others, and endorsed by much of the evangelical world, is based upon a double error. First and foremost it is wrong theologically, fundamentally distorting the meaning of the gospel. But it is equally wrong in its naive assessment of the redistribution of wealth and its consequences. The answer is not some kind of socialistic or egalitarian redistribution. This would be much more unjust and oppressive than our own system, imperfect though it is. To understand this all we need to do is look at the repressive societies which have resulted from attempts to radically redistribute wealth along socialistic or egalitarian lines. Every attempt at radical redistribution has wrecked the economy and the culture of the country where it was tried, and every Marxist revolution has ended in a blood bath. It has left the people with less, not more, as well as putting them under a totalitarian government. In this respect the comments of economist and historian Herbert Schlossberg are very helpful. Schlossberg points out the "hatred in principle" in the statements of the opinion-makers of the day who call for socialistic redistribution:

The hatred revealed in such statements is all that can be expected in a society that has institutionalized envy and uses the term social justice to describe a system of legalized theft. That should alert us to the cant in the old fraud that property rights can somehow be separated from human rights and are inferior to them. There are no societies that are cavalier toward property rights but which safeguard human rights. The state that lays its hand on your purse will lay it on your person. Both are the acts of a government that despises transcendent law.

Those who think they will replace the competition of capitalism with the cooperation of socialism know nothing of either. . . . Soviet "cooperation" cost by 1959 some 110 million lives. The alternative to free economic activity is not cooperation but coercion.[3]

I would ask you to think back once again to the illustration of the watershed at the beginning of the second chapter. There I mentioned how the snow lying side by side when it melted would end up a thousand miles apart. And we saw how, in the case of Scripture, two views which seemed at first to be fairly close end up in completely different places, with disastrous consequences both for theology and the culture in which we live. Now when we consider evangelical accommodation to the socialistic mentality, we really find the same thing happening. With its call for justice and compassion it sounds at first like it is the same as, or very close to, what Scripture teaches on justice and compassion. Those advocating the socialist mentality try to use all the right evangelical words and avoid any red-flag socialistic rhetoric. But what they are in fact talking about is "another gospel." And when we look more carefully at what is involved, we find that the socialist mentality ends up in a completely different place, with disastrous consequences theologically and in terms of human rights and human life. A socialistic program is not the answer.[4] And when a large section of evangelicalism begins confusing the kingdom of God with a socialistic program,[5] this is sheer accommodation to the world spirit of this age. Our response must be confrontation—loving confrontation but nonetheless confrontation. A line must be drawn.

Three Great Weaknesses

But here again we must be careful and have a proper balance. In taking a stand against the socialistic mentality, we need to be careful not to baptize everything in America's past. This is something which I have stressed over the years beginning with my earliest books and lectures, but it needs to be repeated again. There never has been a golden age in the past. There is no age we can look back to, including the Reformation, or the early church, or early America, that was perfect or fully Christian. There were great weaknesses which as Christians we must reject and then work to redress, and I would mention three of these here.

First there is the matter of race, where there were two kinds of abuse. There was slavery based on race, and also racial prejudice as such. Both practices are wrong, and often both were present when Christians had a stronger influence on the consensus than they now have. And yet the church, as the church, did not speak out sufficiently against them. Sadly, Americans indulged in the lie that the black man was not a person and could therefore be treated as a thing. It is remarkable that exactly the same argument was used in the *Roe* v. *Wade* decision of 1973 to legalize abortion. One hundred and fifty years ago the black man could be enslaved because he was not legally a person; in the last ten years twelve million unborn children have been killed because the Supreme Court decided that they are not persons. As Christians, by identification with our forebears, we must acknowledge this wrong and twisted view of race and beyond this make every effort to eliminate racial prejudice today. We can be grateful for Christian men like Shaftesbury, Wilberforce, and Wesley who, on the basis of the biblical view that there are absolutes, could say that these evils and injustices are absolutely wrong. But we can hardly sit in judgment of past generations if the same lie is used in the wanton destruction of human life today.[6]

Second, there is the question of the compassionate use of wealth. As I have stressed in the past, this means two things: first, making it with justice; and then using it with real compassion. As a matter of fact, I have said a number of times and places where I hope it counted that I think when Christians get to heaven and they speak of how much they gave to missions, to build schools, and so on, that the Lord is going to tell them it would have been better if they had had less money to give and had made their money with justice.

Third, there is the danger of confusing Christianity with the country. In this area I have stressed first that we must not wrap Christianity in our country's flag,[7] and second that we must protest the notion of "manifest destiny" that would permit our nation to do anything it chooses. We are responsible for all that we do and all that God has given to us, and if we trample on his great gifts we will one day know his judgment.[8]

The Devaluation of History

After acknowledging these grave weaknesses, we must nonetheless recognize that Christianity did in fact have a profoundly positive influence in shaping this country. When historians devaluate too far the Christian influence in founding the country it is neither good history nor honoring to God for the good things which came out of this influence and especially out of Reformation

Christianity. There was a massive amount of biblical knowledge in the country in that day which existed in general and especially out of the Great Awakening. This did have a profound influence, and many secular historians agree that there was a general Christian consensus or ethos.

But this is not to be so foolish as to think that all the founders of the United States were Christians. They were not. Everyone knows, for example, that Jefferson was a deist. But even as a deist he knew that a God existed, and this made a drastic difference in how he understood the world. In particular it meant that Jefferson grounded the concept of inalienable rights in the Creator. Even if the concept was defective in Jefferson's case, for example, there is a drastic difference between this and the ideas of the Enlightenment, which produced the wholesale slaughter of the French and Russian Revolutions. Or there is the example of John Witherspoon, the Presbyterian minister and president of what is now Princeton University and the only pastor to sign the Declaration of Independence. He was not always consistent in his thinking, as none of us are. But it is most striking to note what the issue was when, in a sermon, Witherspoon openly named and attacked Thomas Paine, the "Enlightenment man." Witherspoon directly challenged Paine's Enlightenment views concerning the perfectibility of man, contrasting this with the biblical view of the fall and the lostness of man and therefore the lack of perfection in all realms of government.[9] Witherspoon was not always correct in his political views. But his Christianity did make a difference in his understanding of the political realities of the day.

But there are those within evangelical circles today who would, under the guise of scholarship, belittle all of this and act as though the Christian consensus was always in a total muddle. Just how far this can be taken may be shown by the example of

one Christian historian who carries the muddle all the way back
to the Reformation itself. Thus he writes:

> [Schaeffer's] confusion rests on his inability to see
> Protestantism as the religious form of Renaissance hu-
> manism. To be sure, Protestants *said* that their con-
> sciences were informed by the Bible, on which authority
> alone rested ("*sola scriptura*"). Yet we all know of
> Protestant inability to agree on what the Bible said, or
> even on what kind of a book it is.
>   In his triumphalism, Schaeffer cannot see the
> ironic and tragic in the Protestant movement, because
> he refuses to see it as an aspect of the humanist move-
> ment itself. In his various works Schaeffer repeatedly
> invokes the Reformation as the answer to the problem
> of humanism, when in reality it is part of the problem.[10]

Do you understand what is being said here? The significance of the Reformation is completely devalued and subordinated to humanism. The Reformation and the Reformers' view
of *sola scriptura*—the Bible as the sole basis for Christian truth—
is thrown out completely. Everything the Reformation stood for
is swallowed up in a morass of synthesis and relativity. Exactly
the same line is taken by the relativistic, non-Christian, secularized historians of our day. This is not a dispute over the facts of
history; in fact, many non-Christian historians would disagree with
this radically disparaging view of Reformation ideas. What we
have here is the infiltration of thoroughly secularized thinking
presented as if it were evangelical scholarship. Yes, we must stand
against those who would naively baptize all in the past and that
would wrap Christianity in the country's flag. But we must equally
stand against those who would accommodate to the world spirit
of this age under the guise of scholarship, and in the process not
only distort the facts of history but Christian truth as well.[11]

Academic Infiltration

Sadly we must say that in the area of scholarship the evangelical world has not done well. In every academic discipline the temptation and pressure to accommodate is overwhelming. Evangelicals were right in their rejection of a poor pietism which shut Christianity up into a very narrow area of spiritual life. Evangelicals were right in emphasizing the Lordship of Christ over all areas of culture—art, philosophy, society, government, academics, and so on. But then what happened? Many young evangelicals heard this message, went out into the academic world, and earned their undergraduate and graduate degrees from the finest secular schools. But something happened in the process. In the midst of totally humanistic colleges and universities, and a totally humanistic orientation in the academic disciplines, many of these young evangelicals began to be infiltrated by the anti-Christian world view which dominated the thinking of their colleges and professors. In the process, any distinctively evangelical Christian point of view was accommodated to the secularistic thinking in their discipline and to the surrounding world spirit of our age.[12] To make the cycle complete, many of these have now returned to teach at evangelical colleges where what they present in their classes has very little that is distinctively Christian.

Note that this criticism is not a call for intellectual retreat and a new anti-intellectualism. Evangelical Christians should be better scholars than non-Christians because they know that there is truth in contrast to the relativism and narrow reductionism of every discipline. But too often Christians have naively entered the academic world with a glassy-eyed fascination and left their critical judgment and Christian truth behind.

The battle we are in rages most intensely in the academic world. Every academic discipline has dominated secularist thinking—especially in the behavioral sciences, the humanities, and the arts. Part of our task as Christians is to carefully understand and study these areas—but then to respond critically from a distinctively Christian point of view. But note, as I pointed out in the preceding chapter, this involves two things: 1) being truly Bible-believing; and 2) facing the results of the surrounding wrong world view with loving, but definite confrontation. Please do not take this lightly. We cannot retreat and shut Christianity up to a narrow view of spirituality; but in the totally secularistic academic world the dangers and the temptations are profound. It is very difficult to live in this world as a college or university student for four years or longer and not become infiltrated by the surrounding world view. And if one is a teacher, the dangers go far beyond this with the overwhelming pressure to compromise one's thinking in order to gain scholarly respectability within disciplines dominated by secularist thinking.

And for those who are professors at evangelical Christian colleges, the responsibility is awesome. Yes, you must clearly and carefully present the full range of learning in your discipline. But this is barely the beginning of your responsibility. Will you then go on to explain the points at which there are fundamental conflicts between the ideas in your discipline and biblical truth? Or will you—in the name of academic freedom, or tolerance, or neutrality—let it all slip by without confrontation? This is not the way the world works. The Marxist sociology professor at the secular university is not interested in neutrality, but will make sure that his ideological position gets across in the classroom. Again I would say, in the area of academic scholarship the evangelical world has often failed to take a clear stand. This of course has not been true of everyone, and we can be thankful for those who have taken a stand. But there has been and is a growing accommodation to the spirit of the age as it finds expression in the various disciplines. And because of this, how many will have come to our schools looking for the bread of life, and leave with only a handful of pebbles? This danger is present in the colleges which are thought of as the best Christian colleges. The problem is not future but present.

False Prophecy

Accommodation, accommodation. How the mindset of accommodation grows and expands. It can be seen once again in the new evangelical call for participation in the World Council of Churches (WCC). It is ironic that just when the secular press was exposing the hypocrisy of the WCC and severely criticizing it, evangelical leaders and influential evangelical publications were praising it. Because it shows such remarkable perception, I will quote at length from *Time*'s article entitled "The Curious Politics of Ecumenism":

> To many conservative Christians in Western Europe and the U.S., the World Council of Churches, an umbrella organization for 301 Protestant and Orthodox denominations with more than 400 million members, appears to be an ecclesiastical clone of the United Nations. Responsive to the growing influence of churches in the Third World, the council has seemingly evolved into a forum for relentless denunciations of the sins of American policy and capitalism. Meanwhile, the WCC has what some critics call a see-no-evil policy toward Communist regimes. . . .
>
> The WCC's sixth assembly at the University of British Columbia in Vancouver, which was attended by 838 delegates from 100 countries as well as thousands of visitors, did nothing to dispel the suspicions of anti-Western bias. For example, a committee headed by William P. Thompson, one of the two top leaders of the Presbyterian Church (U.S.), was responsible for drafting last week's formal statement on Afghanistan. Working closely with delegates from Soviet churches, the committee produced a muted document that asked

for withdrawal of Soviet troops as part of an overall political settlement; that was one of the few times the U.S.S.R. has been named specifically in a political declaration by the WCC. But the statement also said in effect that Soviet troops should be allowed to stay in Afghanistan until such a settlement is reached, and recommended that aid to the anti-Communist Afghan rebels be cut off. Thompson's committee also produced a harshly worded attack on U.S. Central American policy. The document praised "the life-affirming achievements" of the Nicaraguan government; Cuba was mentioned not at all.

Bishop Alexander Malik of the Church of Pakistan, a union of Anglican and Protestant bodies, demanded that the Afghanistan statement be sent back to committee for a suitable injection of candor: "If any Western nation were involved, I am sure we would have jumped on it with the strongest language available in the dictionary. The U.S.S.R. has committed a great aggression upon a neighbor, and it must be condemned." Malik's recommendation was rejected after Russian Orthodox Archbishop Kirill warned that any stronger statement would present "terrible difficulties" for his church and would be a "challenge to our loyalty to the ecumenical movement."

This was vintage WCC politics. The council is willing to risk further damage to its image, not only because many Western church leaders agree with the attacks on the policies of the U.S. and its allies, but also because silence is supposedly the price that must be paid to keep Soviet bloc churches in the council. This pragmatic—some would say shortsighted—approach also prevents the WCC from addressing the plight of religious believers in the Soviet Union. The most dramatic event of the last assembly, in Nairobi eight years ago, was the publication of an open letter from two Soviet dissidents, Father Gleb Yakunin and Lev Regelson, claiming that the council had been silent when "the Russian Orthodox Church was half destroyed" in the early 1960's, and pleading for action against Soviet persecution.[13]

Later the same article turns to the topic of witnessing and evangelism. Here *Time* notes that

> There was a flurry of excitement at the assembly involving a nonpolitical document titled "Witnessing in a Divided World." Bishop Per Lonning of the Church of Norway (Lutheran) called it a "dangerous setback," because it showed a "lack of missionary urgency" and did not emphasize the uniqueness of Christianity. Agreeing, the delegates voted nearly unanimously for a revision, but in dealing with a bushel of political statements on everything from nuclear arms (yes to a freeze) to Palestinian rights (an emphatic endorsement), they never had a chance to act on the rewritten statement.[14]

Now contrast this with what our own evangelical leaders and press reported. An article in *Christianity Today* stated:

> Evangelicals have been delighted with the new WCC statement on Mission and Evangelism, which shows influence of evangelical theology in its strong call for proclaiming the gospel and personal conversion to Christ....
> Subjectively, this was one of the great spiritual

experiences of my life. We are dealing with intangibles, but I must report that I have never been among so many supernaturally courteous, gracious Christian people [i.e., the WCC delegates].... Everything seemed dignified by the presence of the Spirit. The only arguments I had in Vancouver were with my fellow evangelicals....

The majority of evangelicals who caucused at the assembly were also enthusiastic, so much so that they produced a statement commending the World Council and inviting evangelicals to add their gifts to the process.[15]

This report went on to discount any Marxist influence, to minimize the Council's being "fuzzy about the uniqueness of salvation in Christ," to defend the Council's call for unilateral disarmament, and in general tried to find some way to make everything that happened at the Vancouver Assembly sound palatable.

Is it possible that the writer of the *Christianity Today* report was at the same WCC Sixth Assembly meeting that *Time* was at? One would think that he would have had at least as much insight into the Assembly as a secular magazine such as *Time*. Again we see that the world often does understand better than an accommodating evangelicalism. It is hard to imagine how this observer could come away with such a naively favorable report—especially if we consider some of the other things that happened at the Vancouver Assembly.

As an example of how far the accommodation has gone, 200 evangelicals, many of whom are prominent leaders in the evangelical world, signed the statement commending the WCC and calling for more evangelical participation. One of the few evangelical leaders at the Assembly who did not sign the statement endorsing the WCC was Dr. Peter Beyerhaus, a professor at the University of Tübingen in Germany. In an alternative statement, Dr. Beyerhaus, who has been a long-time observer of the WCC, reported on the Assembly as follows:

> To see history in a materialistic context is the chief characteristic of Marxist ideology which in the form of the "Theology of the Poor" has found entrance even into the mission documents of Vancouver....
>
> Speakers who represented traditional Christian doctrines [were featured] side by side with others who expounded radical beliefs incompatible with orthodox biblical convictions. One outstanding example was Dr. Dorothee Sölle. She denounced the biblical concept of God and His Lordship, speaking of a "god-movement," and even encouraged her listeners to write "new bibles."
>
> Other speakers encouraged women to make their female experience the starting point of developing a profoundly new theology in which the reverence for the biblically revealed God as our Father is changed into the cult of god-mother.
>
> Non-Christian religions are presented as ways through which Christ Himself gives life to their followers and also speaks to us as Christians. The fear of many that the WCC could move into an increasing syncretism is confirmed by the inclusion of Indian mythology in the worship program...and by the explicit statement by a leading WCC official...that an evangelistic revival endangers our dialogue with other religions.
>
> The credibility of the WCC's claim to be a prophetic voice decrying the oppression of human rights

is damaged once again by the political one-sidedness in which such violations are pointed out only in the non-Marxist world, while serious offenses by socialist states, whose ecumenical representatives are applauded by the Assembly as passionate advocates for peace and justice, are dealt with mildly or passed over in silence. This applies particularly to the harassment of the churches and the persecution of confessing Christians in these areas.

The decisive shortcoming of the Assembly is the lack of a truly biblical diagnosis of mankind's basic predicament: our separation from God through our sin, and of the biblical remedy, our regeneration by the Holy Spirit through repentance and personal faith in Jesus Christ, resulting in the transformation of our present life and in our everlasting fellowship with God. A rather optimistic view of the human nature and our capability to help ourselves is once again leading to a universalistic view of redemption.[16]

Dr. Beyerhaus' statement includes much more than this, all giving evidence of the fundamental incompatability of the WCC program and philosophy with historic, Christian orthodoxy. But note carefully. The issue here is not even whether or not we should be in a denomination which is a member of the World Council. This is a matter of individual conscience (though I could not be in such a denomination). Rather, the real issue concerns discipline as one of the true marks of a true church. And here we now have evangelical leaders abandoning the principle of discipline concerning even the central doctrines of the faith, and calling for evangelicals to be content to remain in denominations which are permanently pluralistic—with a mixture of Bible-believing Christians and those holding even the most extreme views of liberal theology. Having given up any idea or any hope of ever using discipline to purify the church, any amount of heresy and untruth is accepted as normal in the church of Christ. Dr. Beyerhaus' conclusion is very much to the point: "All these observations contribute to our apprehension that the WCC is in danger of becoming a mouthpiece of false prophecy to Christianity."[17]

The New Utopianism

It is interesting to note that within the WCC agenda there is a whole catalog of issues on which the World Council has "come down on the wrong side," and with which the evangelical world has increasingly accommodated. One that I would mention in particular is related to the proper need for Christians to stand against tyranny—from whatever side it might come, right or left. This includes the tyranny that exists in the Soviet bloc, and the extended tyranny that exists around the globe because of the natural expansionist philosophy of Marxism and the Soviet Union. And note that the Soviet system is *totally* based on the same view of final reality which under the name "humanism" is producing the destruction of our own country and our own culture.

This of course also needs balance: I would say again that our country was never perfect—our country was never perfect, and now it is certainly less perfect. It has been years since I have prayed for justice on our country; I pray only for mercy. With all the light we have had and the results of the biblical influence, and then to have trampled on what we have had—we deserve God's judgment. However, this cannot cause us to forget that the Soviet position is even further down the road. Loving our neighbor as we should means, first, doing all we can to help those persecuted by that system now (and especially never minimizing the persecution of our Christian brothers and sisters in the Soviet bloc); and second, not assisting the spread of this oppression to other countries when failing to remember that we live in a fallen world, we then support the contemporary vogue of utopian views on disarmament.

The Bible is clear here: I am to love my neighbor as myself, in the manner needed, in a practical way, in the midst of the fallen world, at my particular point of history. This is why I am not a pacifist. Pacifism in this poor world in which we live—this lost world—means that we desert the people who need our greatest help.

Let me illustrate. I am walking down the street and I come upon a big, burly man beating a tiny tot to death—beating this little girl—beating her—beating her. I plead with him to stop. Suppose he refuses? What does love mean now? Love means that I stop him in any way I can, including hitting him. To me this is not only necessary for humanitarian reasons: it is loyalty to Christ's commands concerning Christian love in a fallen world. What about that little girl? If I desert her to the bully, I have deserted the true meaning of Christian love—responsibility to my neighbor. She, as well as he, is my neighbor.

We have, in the Second World War, the clearest illustration anyone could ask for on this point. What about Hitler's terrorism? There was no possible way to stop the awful terror in Hitler's Germany without the use of force. There was no way. As far as I am concerned, this was the necessary outworking of Christian love in the fallen world as it is. The world is an abnormal world. Because of the fall, it is not what God meant it to be. There are many things in this world which grieve us, but we must face them. We never have the luxury of acting in a merely utopian way. Utopian schemes in this fallen world have always brought tragedy. The Bible is never utopian.

We all grieve at any war, and especially at the prospect of nuclear war. But in a fallen world there are many things we grieve over but must nevertheless face. Since World War II, Europeans more than Americans have wanted the protection of nuclear weapons and have demanded this protection. We have arrived at a crazy place, with a wild proliferation of nuclear weapons on both sides. Clearly there must be discussion here, and reduction of this capability if possible. But the fundamental factor has not changed: Europe, even more today than in Winston Churchill's day, would be under the threat of Soviet military and political domination if it were not for the existence of NATO's nuclear weaponry.

In connection with this, it is interesting to note the recent comments of Yves Montand, the French left-wing movie actor. Montand, incidentally, is the husband of Simon Signoret who has been known as the voice of the left for thirty-five years in France, and who has been deep in leftist political activity in Europe. In light of this, Montand's recent statement is remarkable: that the present peace movement and peace demonstrations are more dangerous than Stalin himself.

Unilateral disarmament in this fallen world, especially in the face of aggressive Soviet materialism with its anti-God basis, would be altogether utopian and romantic. It would lead, as utopianism always has in this fallen world, to disaster. It may sound reasonable to talk of a freeze at the present level, or to say, "We won't ever use atomic weapons first." But if we think it through, either of these equals practical unilateral disarmament. It must not be forgotten, in this connection, that a freeze does not impose constraints on existing weapons; no present guarantee of safety would be achieved by such a measure.

One can understand the romanticism of liberal theologians in these matters, since liberalism does not agree with the biblical stress on the fallen nature of this world. One can also understand the pacifism of the "peace churches": they have always taken Christ's command to individuals to turn the other cheek and misguidedly extended it to the state. They ignore the God-given responsibility of the state to protect its people and to stand for justice in a fallen world. Both of these points of view are understandable; but both are mistaken. If they carry the day and determine government policy, then the mistake will become a tragedy.

But when those who call themselves evangelical begin to troop along in the popular, unthinking parade of our day, and begin to be romantic and utopian, it is time to speak openly in opposition. If we accept accommodation at this point, how can we say we love our neighbor?[18]

The Feminist Subversion

There is one final area that I would mention where evangelicals have, with tragic results, accommodated to the world spirit of this age. This has to do with the whole area of marriage, family, sexual morality, feminism, homosexuality, and divorce. I bring these together as one topic because they are all directly related and indeed all are part of one of the most significant aspects of human existence.

The Biblical Pattern.   Why are marriage and these related aspects of human sexuality so important? The Bible teaches that the marriage relationship is not just a human institution, but rather it is in fact a sacred mystery which, when honored, reveals something about the character of God himself. Thus we find the man-woman relationship of marriage is stressed throughout the Scriptures as a picture, an illustration, a type of the wonderful relationship between the individual and Christ, and between the church and Christ. Thus, Ephesians 5:25-32 reads:

> Christ loved the church and gave himself up for her to make her holy, cleansing her by the washing with water through the word, and to present her to himself as a radiant church, without stain or wrinkle or any other blemish, but holy and blameless. In this same way,

husbands ought to love their wives as their own bodies. He who loves his wife loves himself. After all, no
one ever hated his own body, but he feeds and cares
for it, just as Christ does the church—for we are
members of his body. "For this reason a man will leave
his father and mother and be united to his wife, and
the two will become one flesh." This is a profound
mystery—but I am talking about Christ and the church.

Notice how the Word of God very carefully intertwines this
description of the normative marriage relationship with the description of the church's relationship to Christ. The two ideas are
so fused that it is almost impossible to separate them even with,
as it were, an instrument as sharp as a surgeon's scalpel. Thus
we read in Ephesians 5:21-25 and 33:

Submit to one another out of reverence for Christ.
Wives, submit to your husbands as to the Lord. For the
husband is the head of the wife as Christ is the head
of the church, his body, of which he is the Savior. Now
as the church submits to Christ, so also wives should
submit to their husbands in everything. Husbands, love
your wives, just as Christ loved the church and gave
himself up for her....However, each one of you also
must love his wife as he loves himself, and the wife
must respect her husband.

Nor is this an isolated passage, for we find the same image of bride and bridegroom repeatedly in the Old and New Tes-
taments. (See, for example, John 3:28, 29; Romans 7:1-4;
Jeremiah 3:14; 2 Corinthians 11:1, 2 and Revelation 19:6-9.)

Thus the husband-wife relationship in marriage, and the
relationship of the individual and the church to Christ are inti-

mately related. Just as there is a real oneness between the human bride and bridegroom who really love each other, and yet the two personalities are not confused, so in our oneness with Christ, Christ remains Christ and the bride remains the bride. This great understanding of the way Scripture parallels the human man-woman relationship and our union with Christ guides our thinking in two directions. First, it makes us understand the greatness and the wonder and the beauty of marriage; and second, it helps us to understand profoundly something of the relationship between God and his people and between Christ and his church.

Shattered Lives.   Now what has happened to this beautiful picture of marriage in our generation? It has been destroyed. And we must say with tears that the destruction has been nearly as complete in our own evangelical circles. If we look at many of our evangelical leaders and at much of our evangelical literature we find the same destructive views on divorce, extreme feminism, and even homosexuality as we find in the world. Just how far the situation has gone among evangelicals in the area of divorce is illustrated clearly by the following observations and quotes provided by Os Guinness:

> For instance, a Christian conservative writes that the break-up of his marriage was a sad but "healthy new beginning for each of us in our own way." And he continues that he was called by faith like Abraham to leave the security of marriage to embark on a spiritual pilgrimage toward emotional authenticity.
>
> Another writes, "I hope my wife will never divorce me, because I love her with all my heart. But if one day she feels I am minimizing her or making her feel inferior or in any way standing in the light that she needs to become a person God meant her to be, I hope

she'll be free to throw me out even if she's one hundred. There is something more important than our staying married, and it has to do with integrity, personhood, and purpose."

The ultimate in refinement are the disingenuous ones who claim to be *separating out of faithfulness to Christ!* Once this would have meant a Christian husband or wife left by the non-Christian partner because of the faith itself. Now it often means a Christian divorcing another Christian over a Christian issue.

Would you have thought, for example, that a commitment to a simple lifestyle could ever lead to divorce? Yes, one writer urges today, "The split finally comes when one recognizes that this kind of conscience can't be compromised. There are levels of importance and urgency in biblical morality. And Jesus' driving concern for the coming of the Kingdom, as a counter to the culture, far outweighed his concern for the maintenance of family structures. There can be as much sin involved in trying to perpetuate a dead or meaningless relationship as in accepting the brokenness, offering it to God, and going on from there." Disobeying Christ out of faithfulness to Christ! The irony is exquisite.[19]

Yes, there must be balance here too. We must have compassion for the divorced person—and for all of those in the whole range of relationships that are shattered by divorce. But under the guise of love, much of the evangelical world has abandoned any concept of right or wrong in divorce and any pretext of dealing with divorce according to the boundaries established in the Scriptures.

Subversive Influence.   And we cannot talk about divorce without speaking immediately about extreme feminism, for this certainly is one of the largest influences contributing to divorce today. It is interesting to note what the editor of one magazine which calls itself evangelical says about feminism:

> For years, the right has argued that feminism threatens to corrupt Western values and to undermine American institutions. I have never understood their concern; I thought they were just afraid of change.
>
> But increasingly I suspect they are correct. Feminism, at least in some forms, is profoundly subversive.
>
> That's why I like it.[20]

This evangelical editor is right at least in one sense. The world spirit of our age espouses an extremely strong and subversive feminist view which teaches that the home and family are ways of oppressing women; that personal fulfillment and career must come before one's marriage and the needs of children; that housework and child care are demeaning; that it is a waste of one's talents to be a full-time homemaker. All of this, of course, has had a devastating effect upon the family, but just as much upon the whole of society as those who have grown up with deprived family relationships live their shattered lives in the world.[21]

The key to understanding extreme feminism centers around the idea of total equality, or more properly the idea of *equality without distinction.* Here again we must have balance. The Bible does not teach the inequality of men and women. Each person, man or woman, stands equally before God as a person created in his image, and at the same time as a sinner in need of salvation. And because of this, each person, whether male or female, has at the same time both an *infinite equality of worth* before God and one another, and a *total equality of need* for Christ as Savior. But at the same time, this equality is not an equality of monolithic uniformity or "sameness" between men and women. It is an equality which preserves the fundamental differences between the sexes and which allows for the realization and fulfillment of these differences; but at the same time, it affirms everything that men and women have in common—as both being created in the image of God, and as *complementary expressions of his image*. Thus we must affirm two things simultaneously: because men and women are both created in the image of God there is a common equality which has enormous implications for all of life; and because men and women are both created with distinctions as *complementary expressions of the image of God*, this has enormous implications for all of life—in the family, in the church, and in the society as a whole. And in this wonderful complementarity there is an enormous range of diversity. But at the same time, this is not freedom without form. The Bible gives enormous freedom to men and women, but it is freedom within the bounds of biblical truth and within the bounds of what it means to be complementary expressions of the image of God.

In balance, it must also be emphasized that because we are all fallen, men have often corrupted their place by turning it into tyranny. It is part of the husband's responsibility to see that, as far as possible, the wife is fulfilled. This too is part of the biblical form.

In contrast to this marvelous balance, the world spirit in our day would have us aspire to autonomous absolute freedom in the area of male and female relationships—to throw off all form and boundaries in these relationships and especially those boundaries taught in the Scriptures. Thus our age aspires not to biblical equality and complementarity in expressing the image of God, but a monolithic equality which can best be described as *equality without distinction*—that is, without taking into account any differences between men and women and how these affect every area of life. In the end equality without distinction is destructive to both men and women because it does not take into account their true identity and the distinctives as well as the commonalities that are bound up in what it means to be man and woman.

Tragic Consequences.   I have dwelt at length on this because it is an absolutely crucial point. To deny the truth of what it means to be male and female as taught in the Scriptures is to deny something essential about the nature of man and about the character of God and his relationship to man. But this denial has equally tragic consequences for society and human life. If we accept the idea of equality without distinction, we logically must accept the ideas of abortion and homosexuality. For if there are no significant distinctions between men and women, then certainly we cannot condemn homosexual relationships. And if there are no significant distinctions, this fiction can be maintained only by the use of abortion-on-demand as a means of coping with the most profound evidence that distinctions really do exist.

Again we see that an idea which sounds at first so close to a genuinely biblical idea ends up in a completely different place. The idea of absolute, autonomous freedom from God's boundaries flows into the idea of equality without distinction, which flows into the denial of what it truly means to be male and female, which flows into abortion and homosexuality, and the destruction of the home and the family, and ultimately to the destruction of our culture. Once more we must say sadly that the evangelical world has not done well here. There are those who call themselves evangelicals and who are among the evangelical leadership who completely deny the biblical pattern for male and female relationships in the home and church. There are many who accept the idea of equality without distinction and deliberately set aside what the Scriptures teach at this point.[22] And there are others who call themselves evangelical and then affirm the acceptability of homosexuality and even the idea of homosexual "marriage."[23]

Bending the Bible.   But note: this cannot be done without directly denying the authority of Scripture in the area of sexual morality. This is not a dispute over a matter of interpretation; it is a direct and deliberate denial of what the Bible teaches in this area. Some evangelical leaders, in fact, have changed their views about inerrancy as a direct consequence of trying to come to terms with feminism. There is no other word for this than accommodation. It is a direct and deliberate bending of the Bible to conform to the world spirit of our age at the point where the modern spirit conflicts with what the Bible teaches. Another example of this in the area of homosexuality, by an author who calls herself an evangelical, is the following:

> It's true that some Christians insist that homosexuals *can* change how they feel—indeed that they should change. But other Christians have begun questioning that notion—and not just capriciously but after careful Scriptural, theological, historical, and scientific study.[24]

Perhaps unwittingly this author has given a concise description of how accommodation works. First one starts questioning, based upon what the world about us is saying, then one looks at Scripture, then theology, then scientific study—until finally what the Scriptures teach is completely subjected to whatever view is currently accepted by the world. The above author's conclusions reflect this in a remarkably creative way: homosexuality is similar to "handedness." That is, some people are right-handed and some people are left-handed; some people are heterosexual and some people are homosexual. And one is just as good as the other.

It is hard to imagine how far these things have gone. Evangelicalism is deeply infiltrated with the world spirit of our age when it comes to marriage and sexual morality. Few would go so far as the extremes mentioned above. But there are many who quietly tolerate these views and in practice, if not in principle, view the biblical teaching on marriage and order in the home and church as quaint anachronisms which are culturally irrelevant in the modern world. For some the accommodation is conscious and intentional; for many more it involves our unreflective acquiescence to the prevailing spirit of the age. But in either case the results are essentially the same.

Believing God's Word.   Why is this whole area of marriage and sexuality so important? First, because the Bible says that it is and speaks in the strongest terms about those who violate what God has established in this area:

> Do you not know that the wicked will not inherit the kingdom of God? Do not be deceived: neither the sexually immoral nor idolaters nor adulterers nor male prostitutes nor homosexual offenders nor thieves nor the greedy nor drunkards nor slanderers nor swindlers will inherit the kingdom of God. (1 Corinthians 6:9, 10)

And again speaking specifically about homosexuality:

> ... God gave them over to shameful lusts. Even their women exchanged natural relations for unnatural ones. In the same way the men abandoned natural relations with women and were inflamed with lust for one another. Men committed indecent acts with other men, and

received in themselves the due penalty for their perversion. (Romans 1:26, 27)[25]

God condemns sexual sin in the strongest language. This
is not to say that sexual sin is worse than any other sin. And to
be consistent with what the Bible teaches, we must take a strong
stand against every kind of sin. At the same time, we can never
forget that God very strongly condemns sexual sin and he never
allows us to tone down on the condemnation of that sin.

Why is this point so important? The first reason, of course,
is simply because God says so. God is the Creator and the Judge
of the universe; his character is the law of the universe, and when
he tells us a thing is wrong, it *is* wrong.

Second, we must never forget that God has made us in our
relationships to really fulfill that which he made us to be, and
therefore a right sexual relationship is for our good as we are made.
If we do not follow God's pattern for marriage and sexual morality, it will be destructive to us personally and for our society
as a whole.

Third, the denial of God's pattern for marriage and sexual
morality shatters the meaning of God's relationship with his people as illustrated in the Scriptures' teaching on marriage and sexual morality. It is not just a matter of what is right and wrong on
a human level; it is a denial of the truth of God and his relationship to his people. If we do not follow God's pattern, we destroy
the true picture of what a Christian individually and as part of
the church is.

Finally, we must say that this applies in particular to the
order within the family. As we have seen already, the Bible paints
a beautiful picture of the relationship of husband and wife in
marriage, likening this to the relationship between Christ and
the church:

Submit to one another out of reverence for Christ.
Wives, submit to your husbands as to the Lord. For the
husband is the head of the wife as Christ is the head
of the church, his body, of which he is the Savior. Now
as the church submits to Christ, so also wives should
submit to their husbands in everything. Husbands, love
your wives, just as Christ loved the church and gave
himself up for her to make her holy, cleansing her by
the washing with water through the word, and to present her to himself as a radiant church, without stain
or wrinkle or any other blemish, but holy and blame-
less. In this same way, husbands ought to love their
wives as their own bodies. He who loves his wife loves
himself. After all, no one ever hated his own body, but
he feeds and cares for it, just as Christ does the
church—for we are members of his body. "For this
reason a man will leave his father and mother and be
united to his wife, and the two will become one flesh."
This is a profound mystery—but I am talking about
Christ and the church. However, each one of you also
must love his wife as he loves himself, and the wife
must respect her husband. (Ephesians 5:21-33)

This is not oppression, as so many today even in the evangelical world would have us believe. It is a beautiful picture
of what marriage should be, but equally of the love of Christ for
the church. To reject this not only destroys the marriage relationship, but it equally destroys the truth of Christ's unchanging
love for the church and the authority of the Bible in the area of
sexual morality.

CHAPTER 6

The Great Evangelical Disaster

Accommodation, accommodation. How the mindset of accommodation grows and expands. The last sixty years have given birth to a moral disaster, and what have we done? Sadly we must say that the evangelical world has been part of the disaster. More than this, the evangelical response itself has been a disaster. Where is the clear voice speaking to the crucial issues of the day with distinctively biblical, Christian answers? With tears we must say it is not there and that a large segment of the evangelical world has become seduced by the world spirit of this present age. And more than this, we can expect the future to be a further disaster if the evangelical world does not take a stand for biblical truth and morality in the full spectrum of life. *For the evangelical accommodation to the world of our age represents the removal of the last barrier against the breakdown of our culture.* And with the final removal of this barrier will come social chaos and the rise of authoritarianism in some form to restore social order.

141

Worldliness

Whether we see this as the judgment of God (which surely it is) or the inevitable results of social chaos makes little difference. Unless the mentality of accommodation within the evangelical world changes, this is surely what we can expect. This will certainly mean that the fiction of a united evangelicalism will have to be faced with honesty, and some will have the courage to draw a line—drawing a line lovingly, and drawing a line publicly. There must be loving confrontation, but confrontation. This also means not accommodating to the form that the world spirit takes today as it rolls on with no limits, claiming to be autonomous. In contrast to this, the Bible offers true freedom with form and a way of life which meets the deepest human needs. The Bible gives not just moral limits but absolutes and truth in regard to the whole spectrum of life.

This next sentence is crucial. *To accommodate to the world spirit about us in our age is the most gross form of worldliness in the proper definition of the word.* And unhappily, today we must say that in general the evangelical establishment has been accommodating to the forms of the world spirit as it finds expression in our day. I would say this with tears—and we must not in any way give up hoping and praying. We must with regret remember that many of those with whom we have a basic disagreement over these issues of accommodation are brothers and sisters in Christ. But in the most basic sense, the evangelical establishment has become deeply worldly.[1]

Confrontation

All that I have said in my book *The Mark of the Christian* and in the preceding chapters of this book must stand.[2] We must indeed give a practical demonstration of love in the midst of the differences. But at the same time God's truth and the work of Christ's church both insist that *truth demands loving confrontation, but confrontation.* And know that it is not as if we are talking about minor differences. The differences are already there in the evangelical world, and trying to cover them over is neither faithfulness to truth nor faithfulness to love.

There are three possible positions: 1) unloving confrontation; 2) no confrontation; and 3) loving confrontation. Only the third is biblical. And there must be a hierarchy of priorities. All things may be important, but all are not on the same level of needing confrontation at a given time and place. The chasm is: not conforming to the world spirit of autonomous freedom in our age and obedience to God's Word. And this means living in obedience to the full inerrant authority of the Bible in the crucial moral and social issues of the day just as much as in the area of doctrine. Obedience to God's Word is the watershed. And the failure of the evangelical world to take a clear and distinctively biblical stand on the crucial issues of the day can only be seen as a failure to live under the full authority of God's Word in the full spectrum of life.

Yes, there must be balance and holiness standing together with love. But that does not mean constant and growing accommodation and compromise—moving along step by step, fitting into the world's position in our day. It does not mean pretending that there is such a thing as a unified evangelicalism. Evangelicalism is already divided at the point of the watershed. And the two halves will end up miles apart. If truth is indeed truth, it stands in antithesis to nontruth. This must be practiced in both teaching and practical action. A line must be drawn.

The Weapon of Connotations

Now we come back to where we started this part of the book, with names and issues: I used to shift away uncomfortably when I was called a "fundamentalist," because of the negative connotation which had become attached to it. But now it seems that

as soon as one stands in confrontation against that which is un-
biblical (instead of accommodation), as soon as one takes such
a stand, one is automatically labeled "fundamentalist." That is
the way Kenneth Woodward used it in *Newsweek*—as a putdown. And when Bible-believing Christians who are brothers and
sisters in Christ get taken in this way by the connotation of words,
it is much sadder.[3]

Let us also think of the term "The New Right." There is
an extreme right to be leaned against. But this term "The New
Right" too has become a term with a negative connotation and
is used as a putdown. When one examines this, it too is usually
not defined and often seems to refer to anyone who is ready to
stand against the slide in our day rather than going along with
accommodation. But note. If it is fair to talk of "The New Right"
and the religious "Right Wing," then it must be equally fair to
speak of the religious "Left Wing"—concerning those within
evangelicalism who have accommodated to the dominant form of
the world spirit of our day. I have not done so, for I dislike the
name-calling attacks which some have used, instead of dealing
with facts and content as I have tried to do. But if I had used
"Left Wing" to discredit what I have been describing, it would
not have been unfair.

I would say again there must be balance. Our country never
was fully Christian, but it was different from that which grew out
of the world view of the French Revolution and the Russian Revolution. And up until the lifetime of many who will read this book,
it was vastly different than it is today—because there was the clear
influence of a Christian consensus or ethos. Certainly what I have
stressed many times is correct: merely being conservative is no
better than being nonconservative *per se*. Conservative humanism is no better than liberal humanism; authoritarianism from the
left is no better than authoritarianism from the right. What is wrong
is wrong, no matter what tag is placed on it.

But with the term "The New Right," as it is often used today—and too often by Christians—it seems to mean that on all the issues we have spoken of in this chapter, there is a willingness to take a stand (even to have balanced and loving confrontation) rather than the automatic mentality of accommodation. And if this is so, we must not shy away from the issues merely because some would use the weapon of connotations against us, especially when these terms can have the possibility of meaning something quite different when analyzed. A sensible person must conclude that all such terms can mean different things as used in different ways. And then we should go on hoping that our brothers and sisters in Christ who should know better will not use the wrong connotations, without proper definition and analysis. *This is the case whether we do or do not care to use any of these terms in regard to ourselves.* We are to reject what is wrong regardless of tags, not fearing proper confrontation regardless of the tags then applied.

May Day

In closing this chapter, I would ask each one reading this book one final question. If the Christians in this country, and the evangelical leaders in particular, had been in Poland over the last few years instead of in the United States, would they have been on the side of confrontation or on the side of accommodation? Would they have marched in great personal danger in the Constitution Day protests and in the May Day demonstrations? Or would they have been in the ranks of acceptable accommodation? The Polish government is great in using terms with adverse connotations as weapons: "hooligans"; "extremists"! They know how to use names to shut up the people.

I cannot be sure where many Christians in this country would have marched in light of the extent of the accommodation in our country—where there are no bullets, no water cannons, no tear gas, and most rarely any prison sentences.

It does seem to me that evangelical leaders, and every evangelical Christian, have a very special responsibility not to just go along with the "blue-jean syndrome" of not noticing that their attempts to be "with it" so often take the same forms as those who deny the existence or holiness of the living God.

Accommodation leads to accommodation—which leads to accommodation...

PART IV:

CONCLUSION

CHAPTER 7

Radicals For Truth

In September of 1965, when I spoke at Wheaton College for the Spiritual Emphasis Week, my message was "Speaking the Historic Christian Position into the Twentieth Century." At that time the youth rebellion, which began at Berkeley in the early 1960s, was underway. There were those at Wheaton, including the student body president, who were called "rebels," and the administration was having problems with them. However, it was this radical group who understood my message that if Christianity is true, it touches all life, and that it is a radical voice in the modern world. The rebels listened. And there were some of them who turned around in their thinking.

We need a revolutionary message in the midst of today's relativistic thinking. By revolutionary, or radical, I mean standing against the all-pervasive form which the world spirit has taken in our day. This is the real meaning of radical.

God has given his answers in the Bible—the Bible that is true when it speaks of history and of the cosmos, as well as when it speaks of religious things. And it therefore gives truth concerning all reality. It thus sustains radical rebellion against the relativism and the syncretism which are the hallmark of our own day—whether that syncretism is expressed in secular or religious terminology, including evangelical terminology.

As we have now come to the famed year 1984, what we need in light of the accommodation about us is a generation of radicals for truth and for Christ. We need a young generation and others who will be willing to stand in loving confrontation, but real confrontation, in contrast to the mentality of constant accommodation with the current forms of the world spirit as they surround us today, and in contrast to the way in which so much of *evangelicalism* has developed the automatic mentality of accommodation at each successive point.

Evangelicalism has done many things for which we can be greatly thankful. But the mentality of accommodation is indeed a disaster. We should note, however, that in holding to the same Bible principles, there could come a time when we will have to lean against an opposite swing of the pendulum. In this fallen world, things constantly swing like a pendulum, from being wrong in one extreme way to being wrong in another extreme. The devil never gives us the luxury of fighting on only one front, and this will always be the case.

However, the problem of evangelical accommodation, in the years we have been considering, and especially at this crucial moment in history, is that the evangelical accommodation has constantly been in one direction—that is, to accommodate with whatever is in vogue with the form of the world spirit which is dominant today. It is this same world spirit which is destroying both church and society. Balance must be considered constantly. But the accommodation we have been speaking of has constantly taken the form of giving in to the humanistic, secular consensus which is the dominant destructive force of our day. And if no change in this comes, our opportunity will be past. Not only will the compromising portion of evangelicalism go down in collapse, all of us will be carried down with it.

We cannot think that all of this is unrelated to us. It will all come crashing down unless you and I and each one of us who loves the Lord and his church are willing to act. And so I challenge you. I call for Christian radicals, and especially young Christian radicals, to stand up in loving confrontation, but confrontation—looking to the living Christ moment by moment for strength—in loving confrontation with all that is wrong and destructive in the church, our culture, and the state.

If there is not loving confrontation, but courageous confrontation, and if we do not have the courage to draw lines even when we wish we did not have to, then history will look back at this time as the time when certain "evangelical colleges" went the way of Harvard and Yale, when certain "evangelical seminaries" went the way of Union Seminary in New York, and the time when other "evangelical organizations" were lost to Christ's cause—forever.

PART V

APPENDIX

CHAPTER 8

The Mark of the Christian

Through the centuries men have displayed many different symbols to show that they are Christians. They have worn marks in the lapels of their coats, hung chains about their necks, even had special haircuts.

Of course, there is nothing wrong with any of this, if one feels it is his calling. But there is a much better sign—a mark that has not been thought up just as a matter of expediency for use on some special occasion or in some specific era. It is a universal mark that is to last through all the ages of the church till Jesus comes back.

What is this mark?

At the close of his ministry, Jesus looks forward to his death on the cross, the open tomb, and the ascension. Knowing that he is about to leave, Jesus prepares his disciples for what is to come. It is here that he makes clear what will be the distinguishing mark of the Christian:

> Little children, yet a little while I am with you. Ye shall
> seek me; and as I said unto the Jews, Whither I go, ye
> cannot come; so now I say to you. A new command-
> ment I give unto you, That ye love one another; as I
> have loved you, that ye also love one another. By this
> shall all men know that ye are my disciples, if ye have
> love one to another. (John 13:33-35)

This passage reveals the mark that Jesus gives to label a Christian not just in one era or in one locality but at all times and all
places until Jesus returns.

Notice that what he says here is not a description of a fact.
It is a command which includes a condition: "A new commandment I give unto you, That ye love one another; as I have loved
you, that ye love one another . . . that all men know that ye are
my disciples, *if* ye have love one to another." An *if* is involved.
If you obey, you will wear the badge Christ gave. But since this
is a command, it can be violated.

The point is that it is possible to be a Christian without
showing the mark, but if we expect non-Christians to know that
we are Christians, we must show the mark.

Men and Brothers

The command at this point is to love our fellow-Christians, our
brothers. But, of course, we must strike a balance and not forget
the other side of Jesus' teaching: We are to love our fellowmen,
to love *all* men, in fact, as neighbors.

All men bear the image of God. They have value, not because they are redeemed, but because they are God's creation in
God's image. Modern man, who has rejected this, has no clue as
to who he is, and because of this he can find no real value for
himself or for other men. Hence, he downgrades the value of other

men and produces the horrible thing we face today—a sick culture in which men treat men as inhuman, as machines. As Christians, however, we know the value of men.

All men are our neighbors, and we are to love them as ourselves. We are to do this on the basis of creation, even if they are not redeemed, for all men have value because they are made in the image of God. Therefore they are to be loved even at great cost.

This is, of course, the whole point of Jesus' story of the good Samaritan: Because a man is a man, he is to be loved at all cost.

So, when Jesus gives the special command to love our Christian brothers, it does not negate the other command. The two are not antithetical. We are not to choose between loving all men as ourselves and loving the Christian in a special way. The two commands reinforce each other.

If Jesus has commanded so strongly that we love all men as our neighbors, then how important it is especially to love our fellow-Christians. If we are told to love all men as our neighbors—as ourselves—then surely, when it comes to those with whom we have the special bonds as fellow-Christians—having one Father through one Jesus Christ and being indwelt by one Spirit—we can understand how overwhelmingly important it is that all men be able to see an observable love for those with whom we have these special ties. Paul makes the double obligation clear in Galatians 6:10: "As we have therefore opportunity, let us do good unto all men, especially unto them who are of the household of faith." He does not negate the command to do good to all men. But it is still not meaningless to add, "especially unto them who are of the household of faith." This dual goal should be our Christian mentality, the set of our minds; we should be consciously thinking about it and what it means in our one-moment-at-a-time lives. It should be the attitude that governs our outward observable actions.

Very often the true Bible-believing Christian, in his emphasis on two humanities—one lost, one saved—one still standing in rebellion against God, the other having returned to God through Christ—has given a picture of exclusiveness which is ugly.

There are two humanities. That is true. Some men made in the image of God still stand in rebellion against him; some, by the grace of God, have cast themselves upon God's solution.

Nonetheless, there is in another very important sense only one humanity. All men derive from one origin. By creation all men bear the image of God. In this sense all men are of one flesh, one blood.

Hence, the exclusiveness of the two humanities is undergirded by the unity of all men. And Christians are not to love their believing brothers to the exclusion of their nonbelieving fellowmen. That is ugly. We are to have the example of the good Samaritan consciously in mind at all times.

A Delicate Balance

The first commandment is to love the Lord our God with all our heart, soul, and mind. The second commandment bears the universal command to love men. Notice that the second commandment is not just to love Christians. It is far wider than this. We are to love our neighbor as ourselves.

First Thessalonians 3:12 carries the same double emphasis: "And the Lord make you to increase and abound in love one toward another, and toward all men, even as we do toward you." Here the order is reversed. First of all, we are to have love one toward another and then toward all men, but that does not change the double emphasis. Rather, it points up the delicate balance— a balance that is not in practice automatically maintained.

In 1 John 3:11 (written later than the Gospel that bears his name) John says, "For this is the message that ye heard from the beginning, that we should love one another." Years after Christ's death, John, in writing the epistle, calls us back to Christ's original command in John 13. Speaking to the church, John in effect says, "Don't forget this...Don't forget this. This command was given to us by Christ while he was still on the earth. This is to be your mark."

For True Christians Only
If we look again at the command in John 13, we will notice some important things. First of all, this is a command to have a special love to all true Christians, all born-again Christians. From the scriptural viewpoint, not all who call themselves Christians are Christians, and that is especially true in our generation. The meaning of the word *Christian* has been reduced to practically nothing. Surely, there is no word that has been so devalued unless it is the word *God* itself. Central to semantics is the idea that a word as a symbol has no meaning until content is put into it. This is quite correct. Because the word *Christian* as a symbol has been made to mean so little, it has come to mean everything and nothing.

Jesus, however, is talking about loving all true Christians. And this is a command that has two cutting edges, for it means that we must both distinguish true Christians from all pretenders and be sure that we leave no true Christians outside of our consideration. In other words, mere humanists and liberal theologians who continue to use the Christian label or mere church members whose Christian designation is only a formality are not to be accounted true.

But we must be careful of the opposite error. We must include *everyone* who stands in the historic-biblical faith whether or not he is a member of our own party or our own group.

But even if a man is not among the true Christians, we still have the responsibility to love him as our neighbor. So we cannot say, "Now here's somebody that, as far as I can tell, does not stand among the group of true Christians, and therefore I don't have to think of him any more; I can just slough him off." Not at all. He is covered by the second commandment.

The Standard of Quality

The second thing to notice in these verses in John 13 is the quality of the love that is to be our standard. We are to love all Christians "as I," Jesus says, "have loved you." Now think of both the quality and the quantity of Jesus' love toward us. Of course, he is infinite and we are finite; he is God, we are men. Since he is infinite, our love can never be like his, it can never be an infinite love.

Nevertheless, the love he exhibited then and exhibits now is to be our standard. We dare have no lesser standard. We are to love all true Christians as Christ has loved us.

Now immediately, when we say this, either of two things can happen. We can just say, "I see! I see!" and we can make a little flag and write on it, "We Love All Christians!" You can see us trudging along with little flags—all rolled up—"We Love All Christians!"—and at the appropriate moment, we take off all the rubber bands, unzip the cover, and put it up. We wave it as we carry it along—"We Love All Christians!" How ugly!

It can be either this exceedingly ugly thing, as ugly as anything anyone could imagine, or it can be something as profound as anyone could imagine. And if it is to be the latter, it will take a great deal of time, a great deal of conscious talking and writing about it, a great deal of thinking and praying about it on the part of the Bible-believing Christians.

The church is to be a loving church in a dying culture. How, then, is the dying culture going to consider us? Jesus says, "By this shall all men know that ye are my disciples, if ye have love one to another." In the midst of the world, in the midst of our present dying culture, Jesus is giving a right to the world. Upon his authority he gives the world the right to judge whether you and I are born-again Christians on the basis of our observable love toward all Christians.

That's pretty frightening. Jesus turns to the world and says, "I've something to say to you. On the basis of my authority, I give you a right: you may judge whether or not an individual is a Christian on the basis of the love he shows to all Christians." In other words, if people come up to us and cast in our teeth the judgment that we are not Christians because we have not shown love toward other Christians, we must understand that they are only exercising a prerogative which Jesus gave them.

And we must not get angry. If people say, "You don't love other Christians," we must go home, get down on our knees, and ask God whether or not they are right. And if they are, then they have a right to have said what they said.

Failure in Love

We must be very careful at this point, however. We may be true Christians, really born-again Christians, and yet fail in our love toward other Christians. As a matter of fact, to be completely realistic, it is stronger than this. There will be times (and let us say it with tears), there will be times when we will fail in our love toward each other as Christians. In a fallen world, where there is no such thing as perfection until Jesus comes, we know this will be the case. And, of course, when we fail, we must ask God's forgiveness. But Jesus is not here saying that our failure to love all Christians proves that we are not Christians.

Let each of us see this individually for ourselves. If I fail in my love toward Christians, it does not prove I am not a Christian. What Jesus is saying, however, is that, if I do not have the love I should have toward all other Christians, the world has the right to make the judgment that I am not a Christian.

This distinction is imperative. If we fail in our love toward all Christians, we must not tear our heart out as though it were proof that we are lost. No one except Christ himself has ever lived and not failed. If success in love toward our brothers in Christ were to be the standard of whether or not a man is a Christian, then there would be no Christians, because all men have failed. But Jesus gives the world a piece of litmus paper, a reasonable thermometer: There is a mark which, if the world does not see, allows them to conclude, "This man is not a Christian." Of course, the world may be making a wrong judgment because, if the man is truly a Christian, as far as the reality goes, they made a mistake.

It is true that a non-Christian often hides behind what he sees in Christians and then screams, "Hypocrites!" when in reality he is a sinner who will not face the claims of Christ. But that is not what Jesus is talking about here. Here Jesus is talking about our responsibility as individuals and as groups to so love all other true Christians that the world will have no valid reason for saying that we are not Christians.

The Final Apologetic
But there is something even more sober. And to understand it we must look at John 17:21, a verse out of the midst of Christ's high priestly prayer. Jesus prays, "That they all may be one; as thou, Father, art in me, and I in thee, that they also may be one in us: that the world may believe that thou hast sent me." In this, his high priestly prayer, Jesus is praying for the oneness of the church, the oneness that should be found specifically among true Christians. Jesus is not praying for a humanistic, romantic oneness among men in general. Verse 9 makes this clear: "I pray not for the world, but for them which thou hast given me; for they are thine." Jesus here makes a very careful distinction between those who have cast themselves upon him in faith and those who still stand in rebellion. Hence, in the twenty-first verse, when he prays

for oneness, the "they" he is referring to are the true Christians.

Notice, however, that verse 21 says, "that they all may be one...." The emphasis, interestingly enough, is exactly the same as in John 13—not on a part of true Christians, but on all Christians—not that those in certain parties in the church should be one, but that all born-again Christians should be one.

Now comes the sobering part. Jesus goes on in this twenty-first verse to say something that always causes me to cringe. If as Christians we do not cringe, it seems to me we are not very sensitive or very honest, because Jesus here gives us the final apologetic. What is the final apologetic? *"That they all may be one; as thou, Father, art in me, and I in thee, that they also may be one in us: that the world may believe that thou hast sent me."* This is the final apologetic.

In John 13 the point was that if an individual Christian does not show love toward other true Christians, the world has a right to judge that he is not a Christian. Here Jesus is stating something else which is much more cutting, much more profound: We cannot expect the world to believe that the Father sent the Son, that Jesus' claims are true, and that Christianity is true, unless the world sees some reality of the oneness of true Christians.

Now that is frightening. Should we not feel some emotion at this point?

Look at it again. Jesus is not saying that Christians should judge each other (as to their being Christian or not) on this basis. Please notice this with tremendous care. The church is to judge whether a man is a Christian on the basis of his doctrine, the propositional content of his faith, and then his credible profession of faith. When a man comes before a local church that is doing its job, he will be quizzed on the content of what he believes. If, for example, a church is conducting a heresy trial (the New Testament indicates there are to be heresy trials in the church of Christ), the question of heresy will turn on the content of the man's doctrine. The church has a right to judge, in fact it is commanded to judge, a man on the content of what he believes and teaches.

But we cannot expect the world to judge that way, because the world cares nothing about doctrine. And that is especially true in the second half of the twentieth century when, on the basis of their epistomology, men no longer believe even in the possibility of absolute truth. And if we are surrounded by a world which no longer believes in the concept of truth, certainly we cannot expect people to have any interest in whether a man's doctrine is correct or not.

But Jesus did give the mark that will arrest the attention of the world, even the attention of the modern man who says he is just a machine. Because every man is made in the image of God and has, therefore, aspirations for love, there is something that can be in every geographical climate—in every point of time—which cannot fail to arrest his attention.

What is it? The love that true Christians show for each other and not just for their own party.

Honest Answers, Observable Love
Of course as Christians we must not minimize the need to give honest answers to honest questions. We should have an intellectual apologetic. The Bible commands it, and Christ and Paul exemplify it. In the synagogue, in the marketplace, in homes, and in almost every conceivable kind of situation, Jesus and Paul discussed Christianity. It is likewise the Christian's task to be able to give an honest answer to an honest question and then to give it.

Yet, without true Christians loving one another, Christ says the world cannot be expected to listen, even when we give proper answers. Let us be careful, indeed, to spend a lifetime studying to give honest answers. For years the orthodox, evangelical church has done this very poorly. So it is well to spend time learning to answer the questions of men who are about us. But after we have done our best to communicate to a lost world, still we must never forget that the final apologetic which Jesus gives is the observable love of true Christians for true Christians.

While it is not the central consideration that I am dealing with at this time, yet the observable love and oneness among true Christians exhibited before the world must certainly cross all the lines which divide men. The New Testament says, "Neither Greek nor barbarian, neither Jew nor Gentile, neither male nor female."

In the church at Antioch the Christians included Jews and Gentiles and reached all the way from Herod's foster brother to the slaves; and the naturally proud Greek Christian Gentiles of Macedonia showed a practical concern for the material needs of the Christian Jews in Jerusalem. The observable and practical love among true Christians that the world has a right to be able to observe in our day certainly should cut without reservation across such lines as language, nationalities, national frontiers, younger and older, colors of skin, levels of education and economics, accent, line of birth, the class system in any particular locality, dress, short or long hair among whites and African and non-African hairdos among blacks, the wearing of shoes and the nonwearing of shoes, cultural differentiations, and the more traditional and less traditional forms of worship.

If the world does not see this, it will not believe that Christ was sent by the Father. People will not believe only on the basis of the proper answers. The two should not be placed in antithesis. The world must have the proper answers to their honest questions, but at the same time, there must be a oneness in love between all true Christians. This is what is needed if men are to know that Jesus was sent by the Father and that Christianity is true.

False Notions of Unity

Let us be clear, however, about what this oneness is. We can start by eliminating some false notions. First, the oneness that Jesus is talking about is not just organizational oneness. In our generation we have a tremendous push for ecclesiastical oneness. It is in the air—like German measles in a time of epidemic—and it is all about us. Human beings can have all sorts of organizational unity but exhibit to the world no unity at all.

The classic example is the Roman Catholic Church down through the ages. The Roman Catholic Church has had a great external unity—probably the greatest outward organizational unity that has ever been seen in this world, but there have been at the same time titanic and hateful power struggles between the different orders within the one church. Today there is a still greater difference between the classical Roman Catholicism and progressive Roman Catholicism. The Roman Catholic Church still tries to stand in organizational oneness, but there is only organizational unity, for here are two completely different religions, two different concepts of God, two different concepts of truth.

And exactly the same thing is true in the Protestant ecumenical movement. There is an attempt to bring people together organizationally on the basis of Jesus' statement, but there is no real unity, because two completely different religions—biblical Christianity and a "Christianity" which is no Christianity whatsoever—are involved. It is perfectly possible to have organizational unity, to spend a whole lifetime of energy on it, and yet to come nowhere near the realm that Jesus is talking about in John 17.

I do not wish to disparage proper organizational unity on a proper doctrinal basis. But Jesus is here talking about something very different, for there can be a great organizational unity without any oneness at all—even in churches that have fought for purity.

I believe very strongly in the principle and practice of the purity of the visible church, but I have seen churches that have fought for purity and are merely hotbeds of ugliness. No longer is there any observable, loving, personal relationship even in their own midst, let alone with other true Christians.

There is a further reason why one cannot interpret this unity of which Christ speaks as organizational. *All* Christians— "That they all may be one"—are to be one. It is obvious that there can be no organizational unity which could include all born-again Christians everywhere in the world. It is just not possible. For example, there are true, born-again Christians who belong to no organization at all. And what one organization could include those true Christians standing isolated from the outside world by persecution? Obviously organizational unity is not the answer.

There is a second false notion of what this unity involves. This is the view that evangelical Christians have often tried to escape under. Too often the evangelical has said, "Well, of course Jesus is talking here about the mystical union of the invisible church." And then he lets it go at that and does not think about it any more—ever.

In theological terms there are, to be sure, a visible church and an invisible church. The invisible Church is the real Church— in a way, the only church that has a right to be spelled with a capital. Because it is made up of all those who have thrown themselves upon Christ as Savior, it is most important. It is Christ's Church. As soon as I become a Christian, as soon as I throw myself upon Christ, I become a member of this Church, and there is a mystical unity binding me to all other members. True. But this is not what Jesus is talking about in John 13 and John 17, for we cannot break up this unity no matter what we do. Thus, to relate Christ's words to the mystical unity of the invisible Church is to reduce Christ's words to a meaningless phrase.

Third, he is not talking about our positional unity in Christ.

It is true that there is a positional unity in Christ—that as soon as we accept Christ as Savior we have one Lord, one baptism, one birth (the second birth), and we are clothed with Christ's righteousness. But that is not the point here.

Fourth, we have legal unity in Christ, but he is not talking about that. There is a beautiful and wonderful legal unity among all Christians. The Father (the Judge of the universe) forensically declares, on the basis of the finished work of Christ in space, time and history, that the true moral guilt of those who cast themselves upon Christ is gone. In that fact we have a wonderful unity; but that is not what Jesus is talking about here.

It will not do for the evangelical to try to escape into the concept of the invisible Church and these other related unities. To relate these verses in John 13 and 17 merely to the existence of the invisible Church makes Jesus' statement a nonsense statement. We make a mockery of what Jesus is saying unless we understand that he is talking about something visible.

This is the whole point: The world is going to judge whether Jesus has been sent by the Father on the basis of something that is open to observation.

True Oneness

In John 13 and 17, Jesus talks about a real seeable oneness, a practicing oneness, a practical oneness across all lines, among all true Christians.

The Christian really has a double task. He has to practice both God's holiness and God's love. The Christian is to exhibit that God exists as the infinite-personal God; and then he is to exhibit simultaneously God's character of holiness and love. Not his holiness without his love: that is only harshness. Not his love without his holiness: that is only compromise. Anything that an individual Christian or Christian group does that fails to show the simultaneous balance of the holiness of God and the love of God presents to a watching world not a demonstration of the God who exists but a caricature of the God who exists.

According to the Scripture and the teaching of Christ, the love that is shown is to be exceedingly strong. It is not just something you mention in words once in a while.

Visible Love

What, then, does this love mean? How can it be made visible?

First, it means a very simple thing: It means that when I have made a mistake and when I have failed to love my Christian brother, I go to him and say, "I'm sorry." That is first.

It may seem a letdown—that the first thing we speak of should be so simple! But if you think it is easy, you have never tried to practice it.

In our own groups, in our own close Christian communities, even in our families, when we have shown lack of love toward another, we as Christians do not just automatically go and say we are sorry. On even the very simplest level it is never very easy.

It may sound simplistic to start with saying we are sorry and asking forgiveness, but it is not. This is the way of renewed fellowship, whether it is between a husband and wife, a parent and child, within a Christian community, or between groups. When we have shown a lack of love toward the other, we are called by God to go and say, "I'm sorry....I really am sorry."

If I am not willing to say, "I'm sorry," when I have wronged somebody else—especially when I have not loved him— I have not even started to think about the meaning of a Christian oneness which the world can see. The world has a right to question whether I am a Christian. And more than that, let me say it again, if I am not willing to do this very simple thing, the world has a right to question whether Jesus was sent from God and whether Christianity is true.

How well have we consciously practiced this? How often, in the power of the Holy Spirit, have we gone to Christians in our own group and said, "I'm sorry"? How much time have we spent reestablishing contact with those in other groups, saying to them, "I'm sorry for what I've done, what I've said, or what I've written"? How frequently has one group gone to another group with whom it differed and has said, "We're sorry"? It is so important that it is, for all practical purposes, a part of the preaching of the gospel itself. The observable practice of truth and the observable practice of love go hand in hand with the proclamation of the good news of Jesus Christ.

I have observed one thing *among true Christians* in their differences in many countries: What divides and severs true Christian groups and Christians—what leaves a bitterness that can last for twenty, thirty, or forty years (or for fifty or sixty years in a son's memory)—is not the issue of doctrine or belief which caused the differences in the first place. Invariably it is lack of love—and the bitter things that are said by true Christians in the midst of differences. These stick in the mind like glue. And after time passes and the differences between the Christians or the groups appear less than they did, there are still those bitter, bitter things we said in the midst of what we thought was a good and sufficient objective discussion. It is these things—these unloving attitudes and words—that cause the stench that the world can smell in the church of Jesus Christ among those who are really true Christians.

If, when we feel we must disagree as true Christians, we could simply guard our tongues and speak in love, in five or ten years the bitterness could be gone. Instead of that, we leave scars—a curse for generations. Not just a curse in the church, but a curse in the world. Newspaper headlines bear it in our Christian press, and it boils over into the secular press at times— Christians saying such bitter things about other Christians.

The world looks, shrugs its shoulders, and turns away. It has not seen even the beginning of a living church in the midst of a dying culture. It has not seen the beginning of what Jesus indicates is the final apologetic—observable oneness among true Christians who are truly brothers in Christ. Our sharp tongues, the lack of love between us—not the necessary statements of differences that may exist between true Christians—these are what properly trouble the world.

How different this is from the straightforward and direct command of Jesus Christ—to show an observable oneness which may be seen by a watching world!

Forgiveness

But there is more to observable love than saying we are sorry. There must also be open forgiveness. And though it's hard to say, "I'm sorry," it's even harder to forgive. The Bible, however, makes plain that the world must observe a forgiving spirit in the midst of God's people.

In the Lord's prayer, Jesus himself teaches us to pray, "Forgive us our trespasses, as we forgive those who trespass against us." Now this prayer, we must say quickly, is not for salvation. It has nothing to do with being born again, for we are born again on the basis of the finished work of Christ plus nothing. But it does have to do with a Christian's existential, moment-by-moment experiential relationship to God. We need a once-for-all forgiveness at justification, and we need a moment-by-moment forgiveness for our sins on the basis of Christ's work in order to be in open fellowship with God. What the Lord has taught us to pray in the Lord's prayer should make a Christian very sober every day of his life: We are asking the Lord to open to us the experiential realities of fellowship with himself as we forgive others.

Some Christians say that the Lord's prayer is not for this

present era, but most of us would say it is. And yet at the same time we hardly think once in a year about our lack of a forgiving heart in relationship to God's forgiving us. Many Christians rarely or never seem to connect their own lack of reality of fellowship with God with their lack of forgiveness to men, even though they may say the Lord's prayer in a formal way over and over in their weekly Sunday worship services.

We must all continually acknowledge that we do not practice the forgiving heart as we should. And yet the prayer is "Forgive us our debts, our trespasses, as we forgive our debtors." We are to have a forgiving spirit even before the other person expresses regret for his wrong. The Lord's prayer does not suggest that when the other man is sorry, then we are to show a oneness by having a forgiving spirit. Rather, we are called upon to have a forgiving spirit without the other man having made the first step. We may still say that he is wrong, but in the midst of saying that he is wrong, we must be forgiving.

We are to have this forgiving spirit not only toward Christians, but toward all men. But surely if it is toward all men, it is important toward Christians.

Such a forgiving spirit registers an attitude of love toward others. But even though one can call this an attitude, true forgiveness is observable. Believe me, you can look on a man's face and know where he is as far as forgiveness is concerned. And the world is called on to look upon us and see whether we have love across the groups, love across party lines. Do they observe that we say, "I'm sorry," and do they observe a forgiving heart? Let me repeat: Our love will not be perfect, but it must be substantial enough for the world to be able to observe or it does not fit into the structure of the verses in John 13 and 17. And if the world does not observe this among true Christians, the world has a right to make the two awful judgments which these verses indicate: That we are not Christians and that Christ was not sent by the Father.

When Christians Disagree

What happens, then, when we must differ with other brothers in Christ because of the need also to show forth God's holiness either in doctrine or in life? In the matter of life, Paul clearly shows us the balance in 1 and 2 Corinthians. The same thing applies in doctrine as well.

First, in 1 Corinthians 5:1-5 he scolds the Corinthian church for allowing a man in the midst of fornication to stay in the church without discipline. Because of the holiness of God, because of the need to exhibit this holiness to a watching world, and because such judgment on the basis of God's revealed law is right in God's sight, Paul scolds the church for not disciplining the man.

After they have disciplined him, Paul writes again to them in 2 Corinthians 2:6-8 and scolds them because they are not showing love toward him. These two things must stand together.

I am thankful that Paul writes this way in his first letter and his second, for here you see a passage of time. The Corinthians have taken his advice, they have disciplined the Christian, and now Paul writes to them, "You're disciplining him, but why don't you show your love toward him?" He could have gone on and quoted Jesus in saying, "Don't you realize that the surrounding pagans of Corinth have a right to say that Jesus was not sent by the Father because you are not showing love to this man that you properly disciplined?"

A very important question arises at this point: How can we exhibit the oneness Christ commands without sharing in the other man's mistakes? I would suggest a few ways by which we can practice and show this oneness even across the lines where we must differ.

Regret

First, we should never come to such difference with true Christians without regret and without tears. Sounds simple, doesn't it?

Believe me, evangelicals often have not shown it. We rush in, being very, very pleased, it would seem at times, to find other men's mistakes. We build ourselves up by tearing other men down. This can never show a real oneness among Christians.

There is only one kind of man who can fight the Lord's battles in anywhere near a proper way, and that is the man who by nature is unbelligerent. A belligerent man tends to do it because he is belligerent; at least it looks that way. The world must observe that when we must differ with each other as true Christians, we do it not because we love the smell of blood, the smell of the arena, the smell of the bullfight, but because we must for God's sake. If there are tears when we must speak, then something beautiful can be observed.

Second, in proportion to the gravity of what is wrong between true Christians, it is important consciously to exhibit a seeable love to the world. Not all differences among Christians are equal. There are some that are very minor. Others are overwhelmingly important.

The more serious the wrongness is, the more important it is to exhibit the holiness of God, to speak out concerning what is wrong. At the same time, the more serious the differences become, the more important it becomes that we look to the Holy Spirit to enable us to show love to the true Christians with whom we must differ. If it is only a minor difference, showing love does not take much conscious consideration. But where the difference becomes really important, it becomes proportionately more important to speak for God's holiness. And it becomes increasingly important in that place to show the world that we still love each other.

Humanly we function in exactly the opposite direction: In the less important differences we show more love toward true Christians, but as the difference gets into more important areas, we tend to show less love. The reverse must be the case: As the differences among true Christians get greater, we must *con-sciously* love and show a love which has some manifestation the world may see.

So let us consider this: Is my difference with my brother in Christ really crucially important? If so, it is doubly important that I spend time upon my knees asking the Holy Spirit, asking Christ, to do his work through me and my group, that I and we might show love even in this larger difference that we have come to with a brother in Christ or with another group of true Christians.

Costly Love

Third, we must show a *practical* demonstration of love in the midst of the dilemma even when it is costly. The word *love* should not be just a banner. In other words, we must do whatever must be done, at whatever cost, to show this love. We must not say, "I love you," and then—bang, bang, bang!

So often people think that Christianity is only something soft, only a kind of gooey love that loves evil equally with good. This is not the biblical position. The holiness of God is to be exhibited simultaneously with love. We must be careful, therefore, not to say that what is wrong is right, whether it is in the area of doctrine or of life, in our own group or another. Anywhere what is wrong is wrong and we have a responsibility in that situation to say that what is wrong is wrong. But the observable love must be there regardless of the cost.

The Bible does not make these things escapable. First Corinthians 6:1-7 reads,

> Dare any of you, having a matter against another, go
> to law before the unjust [that is, the unsaved people],
> and not before the saints? Do ye not know that the saints
> shall judge the world? and if the world shall be judged
> by you, are ye unworthy to judge the smallest matters?

Know ye not that we shall judge angels? how much more things that pertain to this life? If then ye have judgments of things pertaining to this life, set them to judge who are least esteemed in the church. I speak to your shame. Is it so, that there is not a wise man among you? no, not one that shall be able to judge between his brethren? But brother goeth to law with brother, and that before the unbelievers. Now therefore there is utterly a fault among you, because ye go to law one with another. *Why do ye not rather take wrong? Why do ye not rather suffer yourselves to be defrauded?*

What does this mean? The church is not to let pass what is wrong; but the Christian should suffer practical, monetary loss to show the oneness true Christians should have rather than to go to court against other true Christians, for this would destroy such an observable oneness before the watching world. This is costly love, but it is just such practicing love that can be seen.

Paul is talking about something which is observable, something that is very real: The Christian is to show such love in the midst of a necessary difference with his brother that he is willing to suffer loss—not just monetary loss (though most Christians seem to forget all love and oneness when money gets involved), but whatever loss is involved.

Whatever the specifics are, there is to be a practical demonstration of love appropriate to a particular place. The Bible is a strong and down-to-earth book.

A fourth way we can show and exhibit love without sharing in our brother's mistake is to approach the problem with a desire to solve it, rather than with a desire to win. We all love to win. In fact, there is nobody who loves to win more than the theologian. The history of theology is all too often a long exhibition of a desire to win.

But we should understand that what we are working for in the midst of our difference is a *solution*—a solution that will give God the glory, that will be true to the Bible, but will exhibit the love of God simultaneously with his holiness. What is our attitude as we sit down to talk to our brother or as group meets with group to discuss differences? A desire to come out on top? To play one-up-manship? If there is any desire for love whatsoever, every time we discuss a difference, we will desire a solution and not just that we can be proven right.

The Difference of Differences

A fifth way in which we can show a practicing, observable love to the world without sharing in our brother's mistake is to realize, to keep *consciously* before us and to help each other be aware, that it is easy to compromise and to call what is wrong right, but that it is equally easy to forget to exhibit our oneness in Christ. This attitude must be constantly and consciously developed— talked about and written about in and among our groups and among ourselves as individuals.

In fact, this must be talked about and written about *before* differences arise between true Christians. We have conferences about everything else. Who has ever heard of a conference to consider how true Christians can exhibit in practice a fidelity to the holiness of God and yet simultaneously exhibit in practice a fidelity to the love of God before a watching world? Whoever heard of sermons or writings which carefully present the practice of two principles which at first seem to work against each other: 1) the principle of the practice of the purity of the visible church in regard to doctrine and life and 2) the principle of the practice of an observable love and oneness among *all* true Christians?

If there is no careful preaching and writing about these things, are we so foolish as to think that there will be anything beautiful in practice when differences between true Christians must honestly be faced?

Before a watching world an observable love in the midst of difference will show a difference between Christians' differences and other men's differences. The world may not understand what the Christians are disagreeing about, but they will very quickly understand the difference of our differences from the world's differences if they see us having our differences in an open and observable love on a practical level.

That *is* different. Can you see why Jesus said this was the thing that would arrest the attention of the world? You cannot expect the world to understand doctrinal differences, especially in our day when the existence of true truth and absolutes are considered unthinkable even as concepts.

We cannot expect the world to understand that on the basis of the holiness of God we are having a different kind of difference because we are dealing with God's absolutes. But when they see differences among true Christians who also show an observable unity, this will open the way for them to consider the truth of Christianity and Christ's claim that the Father did send the Son.

As a matter of fact, we have a greater possibility of showing what Jesus is speaking about here in the midst of our differences, than we do if we are not differing. Obviously we ought not to go out looking for differences among Christians: There are enough without looking for more. But even so it is in the midst of a difference that we have our golden opportunity. When everything is going well and we are all standing around in a nice little circle, there is not much to be seen by the world. But when we come to the place where there is a real difference and we exhibit uncompromised principles but at the same time observable love, then there is something that the world can see, something they can use to judge that these really are Christians, and that Jesus has indeed been sent by the Father.

Love in Practice

Let me give two beautiful examples of such observable love. One happened among the Brethren groups in Germany immediately after the last war.

In order to control the church, Hitler commanded the union of all religious groups in Germany, drawing them together by law. The Brethren divided over this issue. Half accepted Hitler's dictum and half refused. The ones who submitted, of course, had a much easier time, but gradually in this organizational oneness with the liberal groups their own doctrinal sharpness and spiritual life withered. On the other hand, the group that stayed out remained spiritually virile, but there was hardly a family in which someone did not die in a German concentration camp.

Now can you imagine the emotional tension? The war is over, and these Christian brothers face each other again. They had the same doctrine and they had worked together for more than a generation. Now what is going to happen? One man remembers that his father died in a concentration camp and knows that these people over here remained safe. But people on the other side have deep personal feelings as well.

Then gradually these brothers came to know that this situation just would not do. A time was appointed when the elders of the two groups could meet together in a certain quiet place. I asked the man who told me this, "What did you do?" And he said, "Well, I'll tell you what we did. We came together, and we set aside several days in which each man would search his own heart." Here was a real difference; the emotions were deeply, deeply stirred. "My father has gone to the concentration camp; my mother was dragged away." These things are not just little pebbles on the beach; they reach into the deep wellsprings of human emotions. But these people understood the command of Christ at this place, and for several days every man did nothing except search his own heart concerning his own failures and the commands of Christ. Then they met together.

I asked the man, "What happened then?"

And he said, "We were just one."

To my mind, this is exactly what Jesus speaks about. The Father has sent the Son!

Divided But One

The principle we are talking about is universal, applicable in all times and places. Let me, then, give you a second illustration—a different practice of the same principle.

I have been waiting for years for a time when two groups of born-again Christians who for good reasons find it impossible to work together separate without saying bitter things against each other. I have long longed for two groups who would continue to show a love to the watching world when they came to the place where organizational unity seemed no longer possible between them.

Theoretically, of course, every local church ought to be able to minister to the whole spectrum of society. But in practice we must acknowledge that in certain places it becomes very difficult. The needs of different segments of society are different.

Recently a problem of this nature arose in a church in a large city in the Midwest in the United States. A number of people attuned to the modern age were going to a certain church, but the pastor gradually concluded that he was not able to preach and minister to the two groups. Some men can, but he personally did not find it possible to minister to the whole spectrum of his congregation—the long-haired ones and the far-out people they brought, and, at the same time, the people of the surrounding neighborhood.

The example of observable love I am going to present now must not be taken as an "of course" situation in our day. In our generation the lack of love can easily cut both ways: A middle-class people can all too easily be snobbish and unloving against the long-haired Christians, and the long-haired Christians can be equally snobbish and unloving against the short-haired Christians.

After trying for a long time to work together, the elders met and decided that they would make two churches. They made it very plain that they were not dividing because their doctrine was different; they were dividing as a matter of practicability. One member of the old session went to the new group. They worked under the whole session to make an orderly transition. Now they have two churches and they are consciously practicing love toward each other.

Here is a lack of organizational unity that is a true love and unity which the world may observe. The Father has sent the Son!

I want to say with all my heart that as we struggle with the proper preaching of the gospel in the midst of the twentieth century, the importance of observable love must come into our message. We must not forget the final apologetic. The world has a right to look upon us as we, as true Christians, come to practical differences and it should be able to observe that we do love each other. Our love must have a form that the world may observe; it must be seeable.

The One True Mark

Let us look again at the biblical texts which so clearly indicate the mark of the Christian:

A new commandment I give unto you, That ye love one another; as I have loved you, that ye also love one another. By this shall all men know that ye are my disciples, if ye have love one to another. (John 13:34, 35)

That they all may be one; as thou, Father, art in me,

and I in thee, that they also may be one in us: that the world may believe that thou hast sent me. (John 17:21)

What then shall we conclude but that as the Samaritan loved the wounded man, we as Christians are called upon to love *all* men as neighbors, loving them as ourselves. Second, that we are to love all true Christian brothers in a way that the world may observe. This means showing love to our brothers in the midst of our differences—great or small—loving our brothers when it costs us something, loving them even under times of tremendous emotional tension, loving them in a way the world can see. In short, we are to practice and exhibit the holiness of God and the love of God, for without this we grieve the Holy Spirit.

Love—and the unity it attests to—is the mark Christ gave Christians to wear before the world. Only with this mark may the world know that Christians are indeed Christians and that Jesus was sent by the Father.

Notes

CHAPTER 1 / What Really Matters?

[1]Henry Grunwald, "*Time* at 60," *Time*. October [60th Anniversary Issue] 1983, p.5.

[2]Roger Rosenblatt, "What Really Mattered?" *Time*. October [60th Anniversary Issue] 1983, pp. 24, 25.

[3]Rosenblatt, p. 25. Emphasis added.

[4]Rosenblatt, p. 26. Emphasis added.

[5]Rosenblatt, p. 27.

[6]The terms "biblical consensus" and "Christian consensus," as used throughout this chapter and the book, need some clarification. In using these terms I do not mean to say that everyone at the time of the Reformation in Northern Europe was truly a Christian; nor, when these terms are used in reference to our own country, that everyone in our country was a genuine Christian. Rather this refers to the fact that the Christian world view, and biblical knowledge in particular, were widely disseminated throughout the culture and were a decisive influence in giving shape to the culture. In other words, at the time of the Reformation and in our country up until the last forty to sixty years, the large majority of people believed in basic Christian truths such as: the existence of God; that Jesus was God's Son; that there is an afterlife; that morality is concerned with what truly is right and wrong (as opposed to relative morality); that God is righteous and will punish those who do wrong; that there truly is evil in the world as a result of the fall; and that the Bible truly is God's Word. In the Reformation countries and in our own country up until the last forty to sixty years, most people believed these things—albeit sometimes only

183

in a vague way and often not in the sense that they personally trusted in Christ as their Savior.

Going back to the founding of the United States, this consensus was crucial. This does not mean that it was a golden age, nor that the Founders were personally Christian, nor that those who were Christians were always consistent in their political thinking. But the concept of a Creator and a Christian consensus or ethos was crucial in their work, and the difference between the American Revolution, as compared to the French and Russian Revolutions, cannot be understood without recognizing the significance of the Christian consensus or ethos.

This vast dissemination of biblical knowledge can properly be called a "biblical consensus," a "Christian consensus" or a "Christian ethos." And it may correctly be stated that this "consensus" had a decisive influence in shaping the culture of the Reformation and the extensions of these cultures in North America, Australia, and New Zealand. We must be careful, however, not to overstate the case and imply that the United States ever was a "Christian nation" in a truly biblical sense of what it means to be a Christian, or that the United States could ever properly be called God's "chosen nation."

Moreover, we must acknowledge that there is no "golden age" in the past to which we can return, and that as a nation we have always been far from perfect. As I have mentioned in the past we have had blind spots and serious shortcomings, particularly in three areas: 1) in the area of race; 2) in the area of the compassionate use of wealth—both in how money is made and how money is used; and 3) in wrongly subscribing to the idea of "manifest destiny" as some have done. But having made all of these qualifications, we must nevertheless acknowledge that insofar as the Northern European countries of the Reformation and the extensions of these countries such as the United States do in fact represent a Christian consensus, this consensus has profoundly shaped these cultures, bringing forth many wonderful blessings across the whole spectrum of life. Moreover, the opposite is also true: insofar as our culture has departed from a Christian consensus, as it has so rapidly over the last forty to sixty years, this has had a devastating effect upon human life and culture, bringing with it a sweeping breakdown in morality and in many other ways as well.

[7]See further, *How Should We Then Live?* in *The Complete Works of Francis Schaeffer*, Vol. V (Westchester, Ill.: Crossway Books, 1982), pp. 243, 244.

[8]See further the way I have developed the material in the next two sections in a slightly different form, for example, in *Death in the City* in *The Complete Works*, Vol. IV, pp. 210-212.

[9]See further, *Death in the City* in *The Complete Works*, Vol. IV, pp. 207-299, especially 209-213.

[10]See the treatment of this in *A Christian Manifesto* in *The Complete Works*, Vol. V, pp. 423-430; in Francis A. Schaeffer, Vladimir Bukovsky, and James Hitchcock, *Who Is For Peace?* (Nashville: Thomas Nelson, 1983), pp. 13-19; and my critique of secular humanism found especially in *The God Who Is There* (*The Complete Works*, Vol. I, pp. 5-202) and in my later work, especially *How Should We Then Live?* and *Whatever Happened to the Human Race?* in *The Complete Works*, Vol. V, pp. 83-227 and pp. 281-419 respectively. See also

the excellent discussions of secular humanism by James Hitchcock, *What Is Secular Humanism? Why Humanism Became Secular and How It Is Changing the World* (Ann Arbor, Mich.: Servant Books, 1982); Herbert Schlossberg, *Idols for Destruction: Christian Faith and Its Confrontation with American Society* (Nashville: Thomas Nelson), esp. chap. 2; and Os Guinness, *The Gravedigger File: Papers on the Subversion of the Modern Church* (Downers Grove, Ill.: InterVarsity Press, 1983).

[11]F. L. Cross, ed., *The Oxford Dictionary of the Christian Church* (London: Oxford University Press, 1958), pp. 104, 105. Note that the quote as it appears in the original text of the *Dictionary* uses the German form of the word *Aufklärung* instead of the English "Enlightenment," and that the English form has been substituted in the quote as it appears here.

[12]J. Gresham Machen, *Christianity and Liberalism* (Grand Rapids, Mich.: Eerdmans, 1924).

[13]See further *The Church Before the Watching World* in *The Complete Works*, Vol. IV, pp. 153-162, and esp. note 2, p. 302.

[14]See further *A Christian Manifesto* in *The Complete Works*, Vol. V, p. 423; and Chapter 1, Note 9 of this book.

[15]See further the way I have developed this in an expanded form in *Whatever Happened...* in *The Complete Works*, Vol. V, pp. 407-410.

[16]In recent years I have been criticized for allegedly having left my earlier concerns as reflected in my earlier books and work, and for allegedly having moved in a new direction. This criticism, however, really is not accurate. A more correct way to look at my work would be to see a continuity from beginning to the end. My earlier books dealt especially with intellectual matters and the area of culture. Then there were the books dealing with the Christian life and the church. My later books have made specific application of my earlier work to the area of law and the society as a whole, especially in relation to the crucial issues of human life and freedom of religious expression. Through all of this there has been my continued interest in evangelism (helping men and women come to know Christ as Savior) and an emphasis upon the Lordship of Christ in the totality of life. Finally I would want to emphasize, from beginning to end, the need to walk daily with the Lord, to study the Word of God, to live a life of prayer, and to show forth the love, compassion, and holiness of our Lord in daily life.

The proper way to view my work is to see my later work as a direct extension and application of my earlier work, and to see that I have not in any way abandoned my earlier concerns. I must admit that since my writing has filled so many pages and covered such a wide range, I do face a problem concerning those who are familiar with only some of my work, or those who would like to give priority of one part over another. I would stress simply that my work needs to be taken as a whole, with continuity from beginning to end. Probably the best way to see this would be to consult my *Complete Works* and read it through from beginning to end.

CHAPTER 2 / Marking the Watershed

[1]There was indeed at least one person who raised a lonely and courageous voice when this seminary began to accept a neo-orthodox view of the Scripture. This was Jay Grimstead, a graduate of the seminary, and I would mention him and honor him for his efforts. Jay Grimstead played a decisive role in founding the International Council on Biblical Inerrancy. The Council was formally organized on May 16, 1977 in Chicago with ten of us present. It still did not have the backing of most of the evangelical leadership, and there was no rush of the evangelical leadership to this cause.

The council was formed specifically for the purpose of defending the historic orthodox position concerning Scripture. Of particular note are the two statements issued by the Council. The first statement, issued in October 1978, is entitled "The Chicago Statement on Biblical Inerrancy." The second statement, issued in November 1982, deals with "Hermeneutics." Both statements are extremely valuable in setting forth first what it means to say that the Bible is without error, and second how this applies to the understanding and interpretation of the Bible. The second statement on hermeneutics presents a remarkably balanced and helpful series of twenty-five "affirmations and denials" concerning how the Scriptures are properly to be studied and interpreted. Together these statements set forth the total integrity of biblical inerrancy.

CHAPTER 3 / The Practice of Truth

[1]See further Bernard Ramm, *Beyond Fundamentalism: The Future of Evangelical Theology* (San Francisco: Harper and Row, 1983), especially pp. 19-22 and 43, 44.

[2]The issue here is not really a question of scholarship. Bible-believing Christians should never be opposed to genuine scholarship in any field. Constantly through the years great Bible-believing scholars have engaged in what is usually called "lower criticism"—the question of what the best Bible text really is. It is natural that biblical Christians should find textual study important, because, since Scripture is propositional communication from God to mankind, obviously we are interested in the very best texts possible. Consequently, Christian scholars have labored through the years in the area of "lower criticism."

"Higher criticism" is quite a different matter. Picking up where lower criticism leaves off, it attempts to determine upon its own subjective basis what is to be accepted and what is to be rejected after the best text has been established. The real difference between liberalism and biblical Christianity is not a matter of scholarship but a matter of presuppositions. Both the old liberalism and the new liberalism operate on a set of presuppositions common to both of them, but different from those of historic, orthodox Christianity.

See further chapter 1 of my book *The Church Before the Watching World* (Downers Grove, Ill.: InterVarsity, 1971), p. 9-34, also my *The Complete Works*, Vol. IV (Westchester, Ill.: Crossway Books, 1982), p. 117-132.

[3]Quoted in George C. Bedell, Leo Sandon, Jr., and Charles T. Wellborn,

Religion in America (New York: Macmillan, 1975), p. 237, emphasis added.

⁴George M. Marsden, *Fundamentalism and American Culture: The Shaping of Twentieth Century Evangelicalism: 1870-1925* (New York: Oxford University Press, 1980), pp. 118, 119.

⁵See further *Eerdmans' Handbook to Christianity in America*, Mark A. Noll et al, eds. (Grand Rapids, Mich: Eerdmans, 1983), p. 379.

⁶See further *The Church Before...*, Chapter 2, p. 35-60; also in *The Complete Works*, Vol. IV, pp. 133-149.

⁷See further *The Church Before...*, Chapter 1, pp. 9-34; also in *The Complete Works*, Vol. IV, pp. 117-132.

CHAPTER 4 / Connotations and Compromise

¹Harold J. Ockenga, "From Fundamentalism, Through New Evangelicalism, to Evangelicalism," p. 36, in Kenneth S. Kantzer, ed., *Evangelical Roots: A Tribute to Wilbur Smith* (Nashville: Thomas Nelson, 1978), p. 36, emphasis added.

²Thomas C. Oden, *Agenda for Theology: Recovering Christian Roots* (San Francisco: Harper and Row, 1979), pp. 29-31, emphasis added. Oden is a very interesting example. He was a thoroughgoing liberal who recognized that liberalism had completely failed, and we can commend him in his courage to say this publicly and decisively. This has led him toward what is essentially a neo-orthodox position, but one that tries at the same time to take the full range of historic Christianity seriously. Since, however, he does not accept the full authority and inerrancy of the Bible he is still left with a serious problem—namely, upon what will he finally base his faith? Without the objective truth of the Bible as his foundation, Oden is still left without any way to appropriate with confidence the truth of the Scriptures, nor really to sort through the mixture of truth and error in the life and theology of the church through the centuries. Thus we can commend Oden for rediscovering the stream of historic orthodoxy, but we must say that his theology is still seriously deficient with regard to his understanding of the authority of the Bible. Without the full authority and inerrancy of the Bible, he is left without any final authority and caught in the same basic problem that he started with. It is interesting to note that the issue which started Oden to reconsider his liberalism was the liberal stance on abortion. Thus Oden comments:

> So when I am speaking of a diarrhea of religious accommodation, I am not thinking of "the other guys" or speaking in the abstract, but out of my own personal history....
>
> The shocker is not merely that I rode every bandwagon in sight, but that I thought I was doing Christian teaching a marvelous favor by it, and at times considered it the very substance of the Christian teaching office....
>
> It was the abortion movement, more than anything else, that brought me to movement revulsiveness. The climbing abortion statistics made me movement weary, movement demoralized. I now

suspect that a fair amount of my own idealistic history of political action was ill conceived by self-deception romanticisms, in search of power in the form of prestige, that were from the beginning willing to destroy human traditions in the name of humanity, and at the end willing to extinguish the futures of countless unborn children in the name of individual autonomy. (pp. 24, 25)

[3]Lance Morrow, "Thinking Animal Thoughts," *Time*. October 3, 1983, p. 86, emphasis added.

[4]David Neff, "Who's Afraid of the Secular Humanists?" *His*. March 1983, pp. 4-7, 31.

[5]See further how I have carefully defined "humanism" in Francis A. Schaeffer, *A Christian Manifesto* (Westchester, Ill.: Crossway Books, 1981), pp. 22-24, in *The Complete Works*, Vol. V (Westchester, Ill.: Crossway Books, 1982), pp. 425-527. On the question of what humanism is, see further James Hitchcock, *What Is Secular Humanism?* (Ann Arbor, Mich.: Servant Books, 1982).

[6]Peter Singer, "Sanctity of Life or Quality of Life?" *Pediatrics*. July 1983, pp. 128, 129.

[7]Once abortion is accepted there is no logical boundary as to how far the devaluation of human life can be taken. Think how quickly there is discussion concerning the use of fetuses for experimentation. It is a horror even to think about. But once the unborn human life is not legally accepted and protected as a person, this is a most logical extension. Concerning the implications of fetal experimentation and documented cases of this see "On Human Experimentation," Donald DeMarco, *The Human Life Review*, Fall 1983, pp. 48-60.

CHAPTER 5 / Forms of the World Spirit

[1]Russ Williams, "Spotlight: Evangelicals for Social Action," *Evangelical Newsletter*. October 15, 1982, p. 4, emphasis added.

[2]For an expanded treatment and an incisive critique of the "socialist mentality" see further Franky Schaeffer, *Bad News for Modern Man* (Westchester, Ill.: Crossway Books, 1984).

[3]Herbert Schlossberg, *Idols for Destruction: Christian Faith and Its Confrontation with American Society* (Nashville: Thomas Nelson, 1983), pp. 133, 134.

Alexander Solzhenitsyn's comments are also instructive here. In an article entitled "Three Key Moments in Japanese History," *National Review*, December 9, 1983, Solzhenitsyn writes:

This is an appropriate place to touch briefly upon a fashionable and widespread myth about socialism. Although this term lacks any precise, unambiguous meaning, it has come to stand, the world over, for some vague dream of a "just society." At the heart of socialism lies the fallacy that all human problems can be solved by social reorganization. But even when socialism promises to take the very mildest of forms, it always attempts to implement by force the contrived and unattainable notion that all people must be equal. One of the most brilliant thinkers in Russia today, physicist Yuri Orlov (now ill and close to death after more than five years' confinement in a Communist labor camp), has demonstrated that *pure* socialism is always and inevitably totalitarian. Orlov shows that it is immaterial how mild and gradual the measures of advancing socialism may be: if they are consistent, then the conveyor-belt-like sequence of socialist reforms will hurl that country (or the entire world) into the abyss of Communist totalitarianism. And totalitarianism is what the physicist calls an "energy well." It is easy to tumble in, but it takes extraordinary effort and exceptional circumstances to effect an escape.

[4]See further the work of John Perkins for an outstanding example of an alternative to the "socialist mentality"—an alternative which is at once biblical, compassionate, and practical. Perkins, who is a black himself, emphasizes the need for blacks to be active in the economic system, to be given opportunity, and to be treated justly, and to build equity within the economic system. See especially John Perkins, *Let Justice Roll Down* (Ventura, Calif.: Regal Books, 1976), *A Quiet Revolution: The Christian Response to Human Need, A Strategy for Today* (Waco, Texas: Word, 1976), and *With Justice For All* (Ventura, Calif.: Regal Books, 1982).

[5]It is interesting to note that while many evangelicals are beginning to sing the praises of socialism, a growing number of secular socialists are growing weary of socialism. Of particular interest is the *"Nouveaux Philsophes,"* Bernard-Henri Levy, whom *The Christian Science Monitor* calls "one of France's greatest contemporary philosophers." Levy is not a Christian by any means, but his insight into the problem of morality, social ethics, and law is remarkable. Levy comments:

> I am not a man of faith but I think if we are looking for a new foundation of ethics, the best ground is the old biblical tradition. These old manuscripts contain the principles of human rights, the idea of individuality, the idea of exile and cosmopolitanism. Marxism maintains there is no absolute ethics, truth, evil, and good; it all depends on the circumstance and the class which is expressing it. If you want, however, to escape this relativity of ethics you'll find the tools and inspiration in the Bible.

Remarkably, Levy sees the total incompatability of Marxism with Christianity better than many evangelical Christians. See further the complete article by Stewart McBride, "'New Philosopher' Bernard-Henri Levy: A French Leftist Takes Out After Socialism." *The Christian Science Monitor* (Pullout Section). January 20, 1983, pp. B1-B3.

[6]See further how I have developed this in *How Should We Then Live?*

(Westchester, Ill.: Crossway Books, 1976), pp. 113, 114 and 127, 128; in *The Complete Works*, Vol. V, p. 141, 142 and pp. 152, 153. I would mention further that in the matter of race, all the way back to the time that I was a pastor in St. Louis in the 1940s and the black neighborhood was getting closer to our church building, I was stressing to my elders that color must *never* be a factor in determining who was to be accepted as a member of the church, and that I would resign as the pastor if it were. And through the years, a number of blacks have found L'Abri to be the first place where race made no difference at all. In the 1940s, many of our leading evangelical schools—and I'm not thinking of schools such as Bob Jones here at all—still held strict racial dating laws and all the rest. I will never forget one black who attended such a school who said at L'Abri, "This is the first place I was treated as a man." When he said it, I wept. I'm glad he could say that.

[7]See further *A Christian Manifesto*, p. 121; and in *The Complete Works*, Vol. V, p. 486.

[8]See further, Francis A. Schaeffer, Vladimir Bukovsky, and James Hitchcock, *Who Is For Peace?* (Nashville: Thomas Nelson, 1983), p. 19.

[9]*Witherspoon's Works*, Vol. 5, p. 184.

[10]Ronald A. Wells, "Francis Schaeffer's Jeremiad," *Reformed Journal*. May 1982, p. 18.

[11]This is not just abstract academic discussion. For if Christian truth makes no or little difference in society (without it ever being a golden age) and if all is only a mixture, including the Reformation concept of *sola scriptura*—if this is only an illusion, then indeed Christianity is only one more piece of data in a world of probability, uncertainty, and constant flux. We should not be surprised that the historian I quoted above (see Note 10) who so devaluated the Reformation and its claim of *sola scriptura* in another article urges evangelicals to look at Walter Rauschenbusch and Reinhold Niebuhr and to their social gospel as our basis of having something to say to modern culture. For those of you who know these two men, you know what this means. The earlier evangelicals saw themselves in complete conflict with Niebuhr's social gospel.

[12]For a personal account of how this can happen, for example in psychology, see the remarkable chapter entitled "Wolf in the Fold" in William Kirk Kilpatrick's book *Psychological Seduction* (Nashville: Thomas Nelson, 1983), pp. 13-27.

[13]Richard N. Ostling, "The Curious Politics of Ecumenism," *Time*. August 22, 1983, p. 46. On the Marxist influence in the WCC contributions to guerilla warfare causes see further: Richard N. Ostling, "Warring Over Where Donations Go," *Time*. March 28, 1983, pp. 58, 59; Kenneth L. Woodward and David Gates, "Ideology Under the Alms," *Newsweek*. February 7, 1983, pp. 61, 62; and Raël Jean Isaac, "Do You Know Where Your Church Offerings Go?" *Readers Digest*. January 1983, pp. 120-125.

[14]Ostling, "The Curious Politics," p. 46.

[15]Richard Lovelace, "Are There Winds of Change at the World Council?" *Christianity Today*. September 16, 1983, pp. 33, 34.

[16]Peter Beyerhaus, Arthur Johnston, and Myung Yuk Kim, "An Evangelical Evaluation of the WCC's Sixth Assembly in Vancouver," as reprinted in

Theological Student Fellowship Bulletin. September-October, 1983, pp. 19, 20.
    [17]Beyerhaus, p. 20.
    [18]For an expanded treatment concerning the related questions of nuclear defense and pacifism see Schaeffer, *Who Is For Peace?*, esp. pp. 19-30. For an excellent treatment in a longer format see Jerram Barrs, *Who Are the Peacemakers? The Christian Case for Nuclear Deterrence* (Westchester, Ill.: Crossway Books, 1983).
    [19]Os Guinness, *The Gravedigger File: Papers on the Subversion of the Modern Church* (Downers Grove, Ill.: InterVarsity Press, 1983), pp. 99, 100, emphasis in the original.
    [20]John F. Alexander, "Feminism as a Subversive Activity," *The Other Side*. July 1982, p. 8.
    [21]It is interesting to note how sociologists Brigitte Berger and Peter L. Berger link the breakdown of the family and the prevailing antifamily attitude in our culture with a whole range of other issues. The Bergers write:

> Those who would do away with the bourgeois family would like, if at all possible, to do away with *all* risks. This fantasy of a risk-free existence expresses itself in some of its central causes; the ideal of the "swinging single," with no ties on his or her project of endless self-realization; the idealization of abortion, once and for all eliminating the vestigial risk of pregnancy in sexual relations; the insistence that a "gay life-style" is as socially legitimate as heterosexual marriage, thereby putting on the same level a relatively risk-free (since childless) relationship with the most risky relationship of all. All these themes can be subsumed under the category of "antinatalism." They can then be seen in a perfectly logical configuration with other ideological themes prevalent in the same strata: *political leftism, zero-growth and zero-population theories, anti-nuclear and more generally anti-technological sentiments, pacifism and a benignly nonaggressive posture in international relations, a deep suspicion of patriotism* (which always has an at least potentially military dimension), *and a generally negative attitude to the values of discipline, achievement, and competitiveness*. In the aggregate, this is indeed a constellation of decadence. A society dominated by these themes has rather poor prospects in the real world, which is mostly inhabited by people with very contrary norms and habits.
>
> We recognize the likelihood that some readers will be offended by the above paragraphs; we certainly do not expect to persuade anyone by such a sketchy argument. We only make it here to indicate that the fate of the bourgeois family *is linked, in our opinion, with much broader questions of the survival chances of contemporary Western societies*. In any case, our defense of the bourgeois family does not necessarily depend on agreement concerning these wider issues. But there is one more point that should be stressed if one places this topic in the framework of decadence:

That is the point that the decadent syndrome is not distributed uni-
formly throughout our societies. Both in North America and in
Western Europe it is concentrated in those strata that we have described as the new "knowledge class" (in the case of evangelicalism this corresponds to the evangelical leadership, especially as
found in evangelical "knowledge industries" such as education and
print media) though it radiates into other strata from this epicenter.
There are other classes (notably the lower-middle and working
classes) and large, relatively unassimilated ethnic groups that are
much less marked by this syndrome and, in some instances, not
touched at all by it. The fate of the bourgeois family (*and, we believe, the future survivability of these societies*) thus hinges on the
future development of these groups. (pp. 135-146, emphasis added)

Or in other words, as this applied to evangelical leadership, the Bergers
are pointing out that the leadership within evangelicalism has accommodated
to the ideas which happen to be in vogue among the secular "knowledge class."
See further the Bergers very insightful book entitled *The War Over the Family:
Capturing the Middle Ground* (New York: Doubleday, 1983).

[22]See for example, Paul K. Jewett, *Man as Male and Female* (Grand Rapids, Mich.: Eerdmans, 1975); and Virginia R. Mollenkott, *Women, Men and
the Bible* (Nashville: Abingdon, 1977).

[23]See for example, Letha Dawson Scanzoni and Virginia R. Mollenkott, *Is
the Homosexual My Neighbor?* (San Francisco: Harper and Row, 1980).

[24]Letha Dawson Scanzoni, "Can Homosexuals Change?" *The Other Side*.
January 1984, p. 14.

[25]See further: 1 Corinthians 6:9, 10; 1 Timothy 1:9, 10; Jude 6, 7; 2 Peter
2:4, 6-8; Leviticus 18:22 and 20:13.

CHAPTER 6 / The Great Evangelical Disaster

[1]Although I would not agree with Richard Quebedeaux in his theology, the
main sociological conclusion he reaches in his influential book *The Worldly
Evangelicals* (San Francisco: Harper and Row, 1978) is very much to the point—
namely, that the leadership of evangelicalism has become worldly in the proper
sense of the word.

[2]See Francis A. Schaeffer, *The Mark of the Christian* (Downers Grove, Ill.:
InterVarsity, 1970); in *The Complete Works*, Vol. IV, pp. 183-205.

[3]Note, for example, the comments of Gill Davis, in "Christians for Socialism," which appeared in *The Other Side*: "I am concerned with those mealy-
mouthed preachers ... In this country, the mythological support for fascism is
often right-wing fundamentalism." As reported in Lloyd Billingsley, "First
Church of Christ Socialist," *National Review*. October 28, 1983, p. 1339.